SUPERNATURAL

Santana

Transcribed by Hemme Luttjeboer

Special thanks to Jorge Santana for his assistance
Project Manager: Aaron Stang
Music Editor: Colgan Bryan
Book Art Layout: Carmen Fortunato
Cover Art: Adapted from Michael Rios' original painting *Mumbo Jumbo*
(poster available from www.santana.com);
Designed by Su. Suttle/www.nekostudios.com
© 1999 River Of Colors™
Back Cover Photo © 1999 Jay Blakesberg

WARNER BROS. PUBLICATIONS - THE GLOBAL LEADER IN PRINT
USA: 15800 NW 48th Avenue, Miami, FL 33014

WARNER/CHAPPELL MUSIC
CANADA: 40 SHEPPARD AVE. WEST, SUITE 800
TORONTO, ONTARIO, M2N 6K9
SCANDINAVIA: P.O. BOX 533, VENDEVAGEN 85 B
S-182 15, DANDERYD, SWEDEN
AUSTRALIA: P.O. BOX 353
3 TALAVERA ROAD, NORTH RYDE N.S.W. 2113

Carisch
NUOVA CARISCH
ITALY: VIA CAMPANIA, 12
20098 S. GIULIANO MILANESE (MI)
ZONA INDUSTRIALE SESTO ULTERIANO
SPAIN: MAGALLANES, 25
28015 MADRID
FRANCE: 20, RUE DE LA VILLE-L'EVEQUE, 75008 PARIS

IMP
INTERNATIONAL MUSIC PUBLICATIONS LIMITED
ENGLAND: GRIFFIN HOUSE,
161 HAMMERSMITH ROAD, LONDON W6 8BS
GERMANY: MARSTALLSTR. 8, D-80539 MUNCHEN
DENMARK: DANMUSIK, VOGNMAGERGADE 7
DK 1120 KOBENHAVNK

Contents

(DA LE) YALEO

Words and Music by
S. MUTELA, H. BASTIEN,
CARLOS SANTANA and C. POLLONI

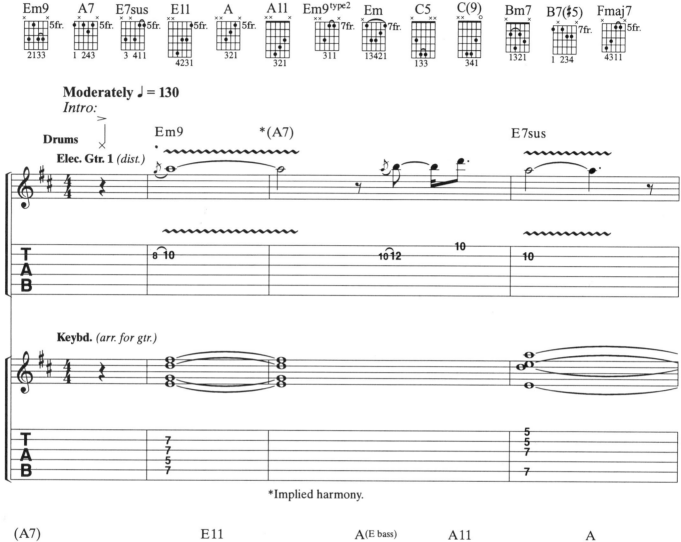

*Implied harmony.

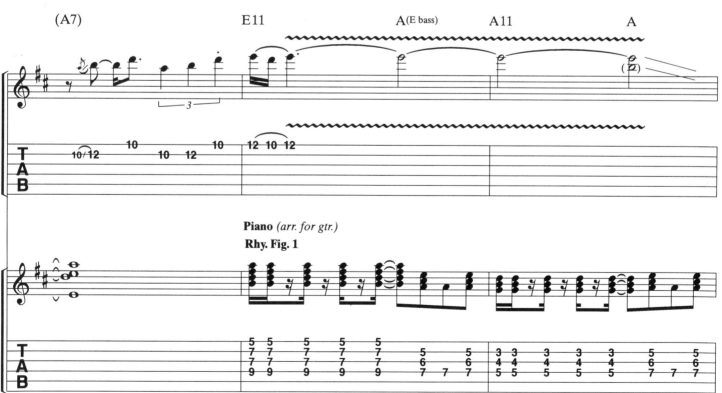

(Da Le) Yaleo - 17 - 1
0413B

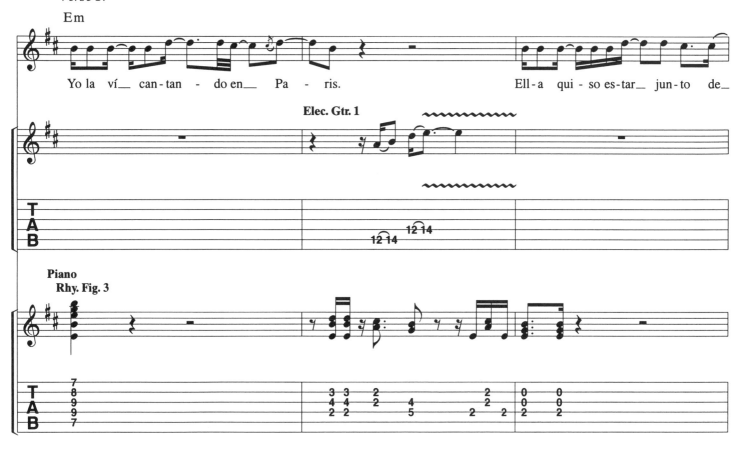

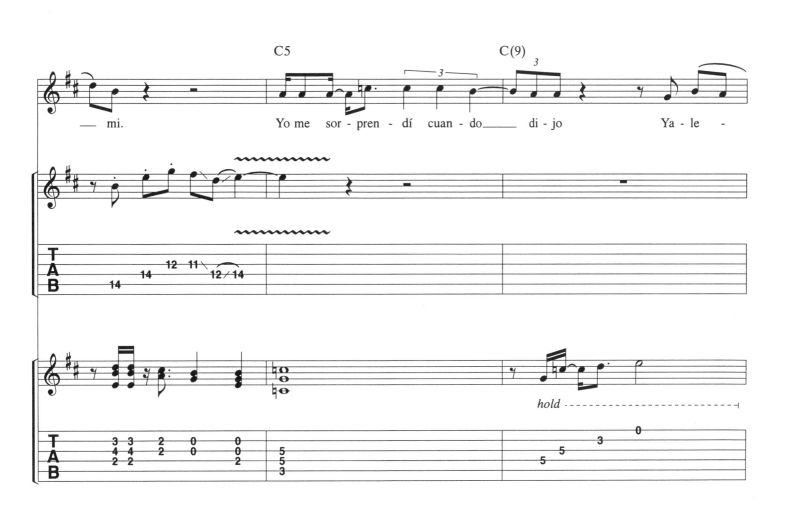

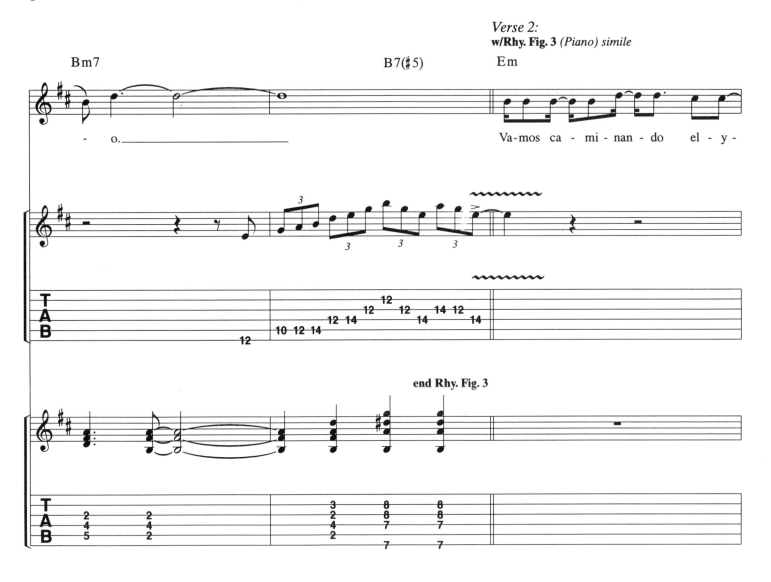

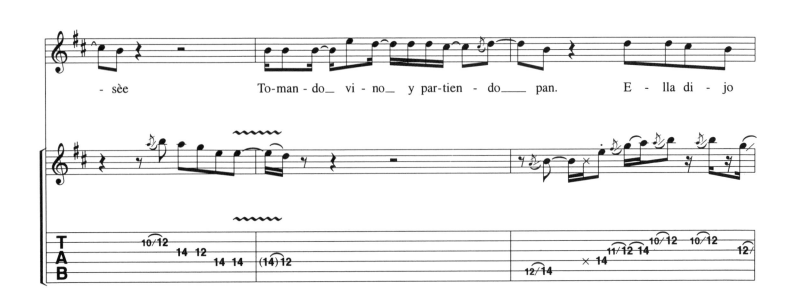

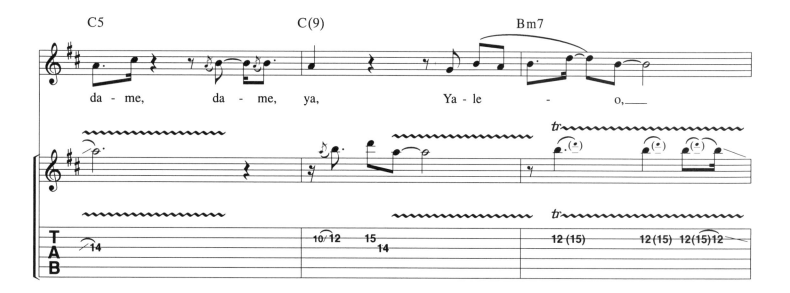

Chorus:
w/Rhy. Fig. 2 *(Piano) 4 times, simile*

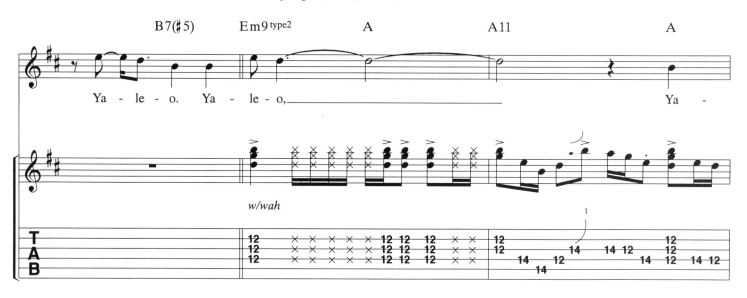

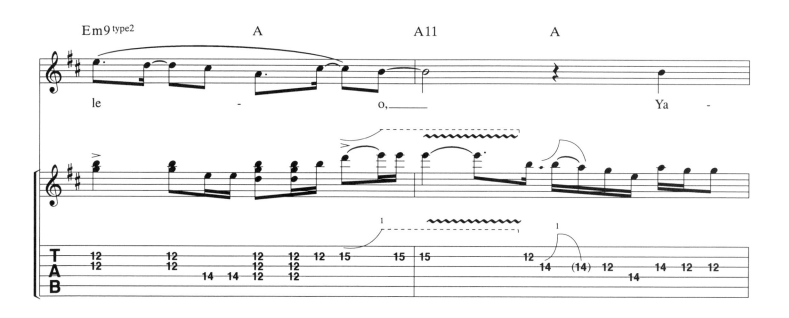

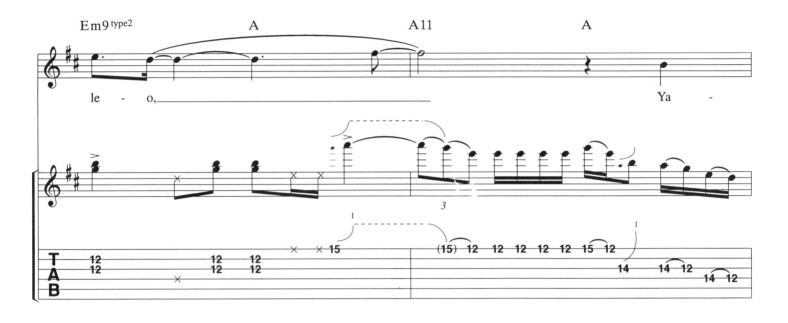

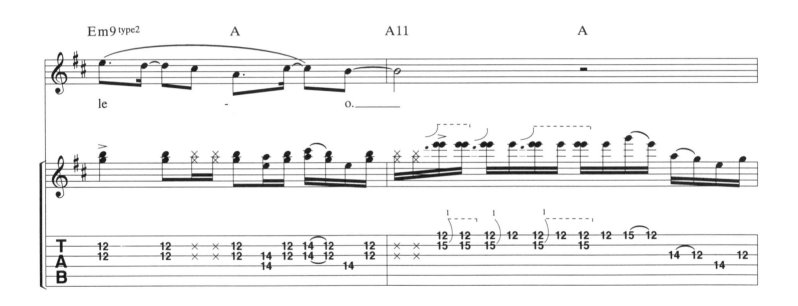

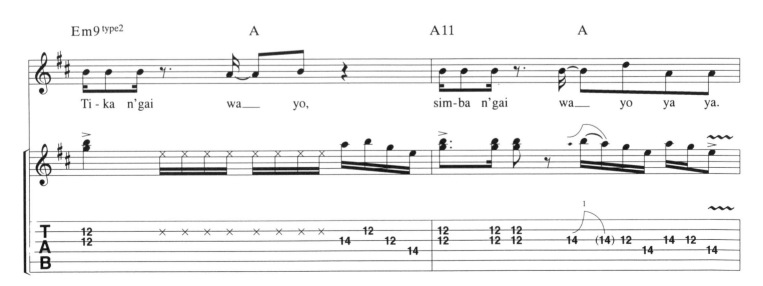

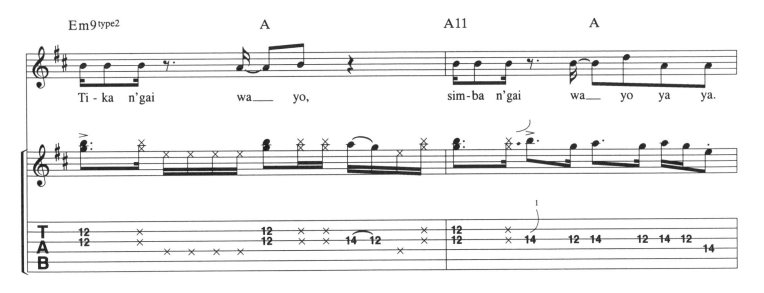

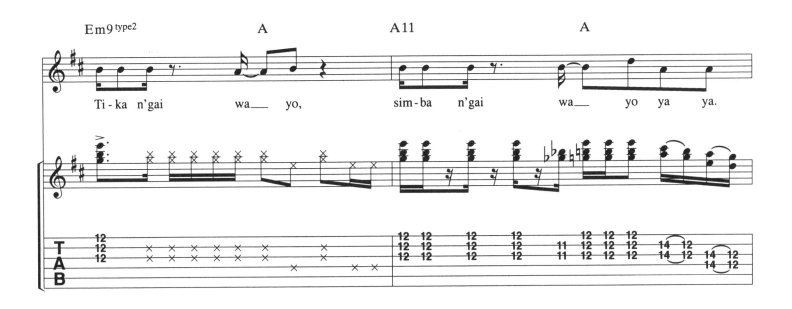

To Coda ⊕

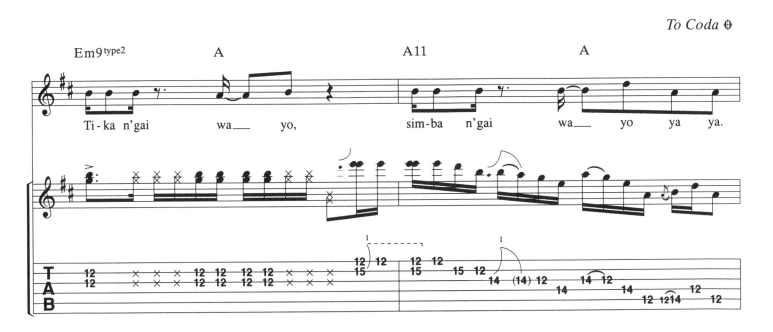

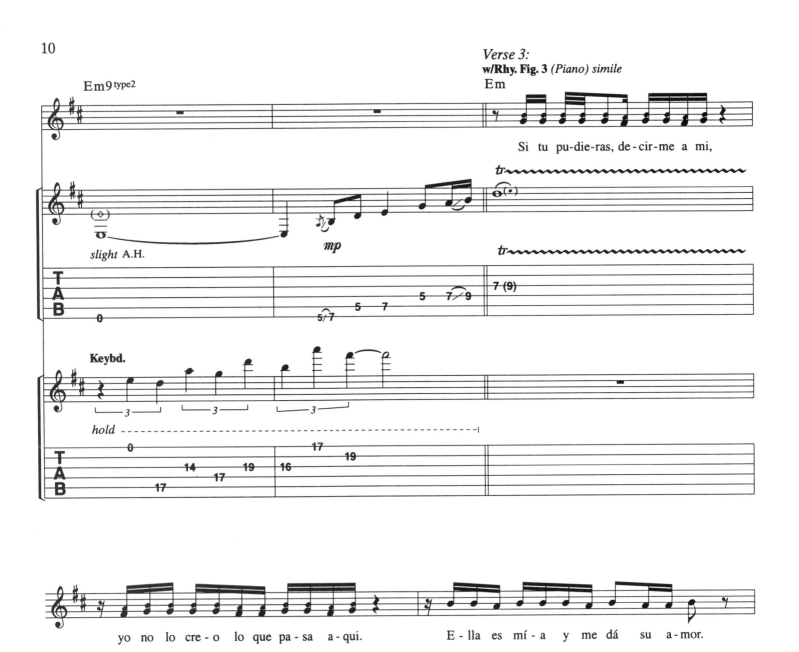

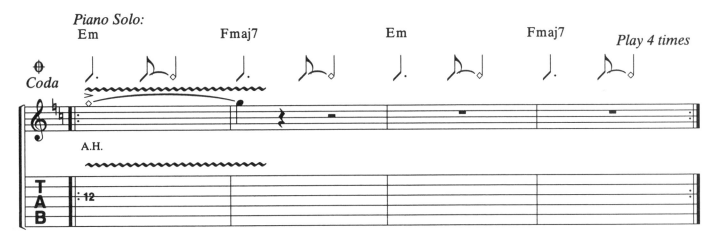

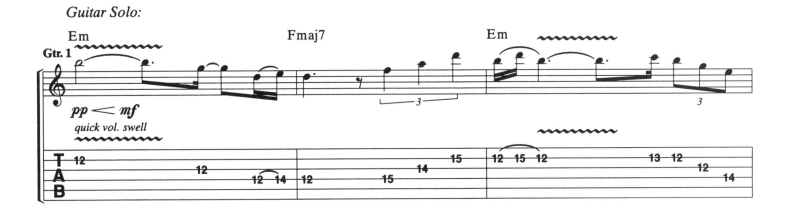

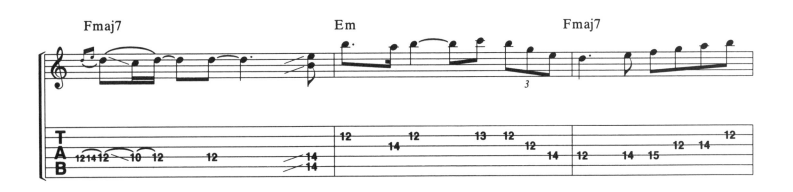

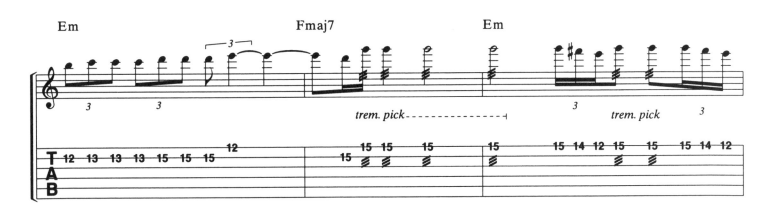

(Da Le) Yaleo - 17 - 9
0413B

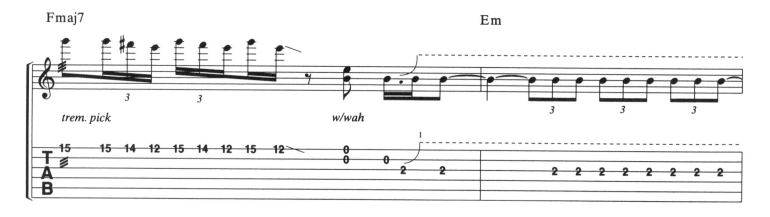

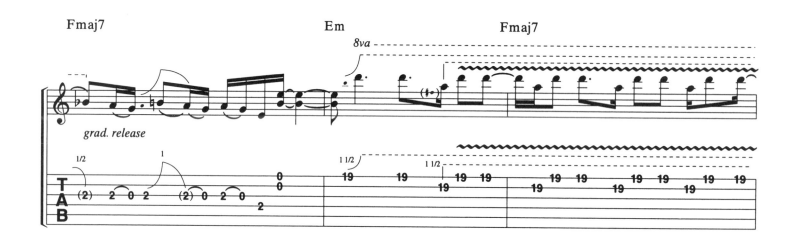

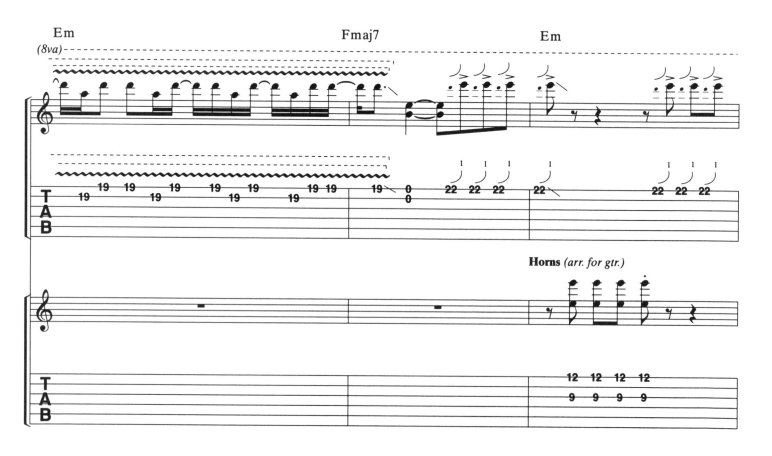

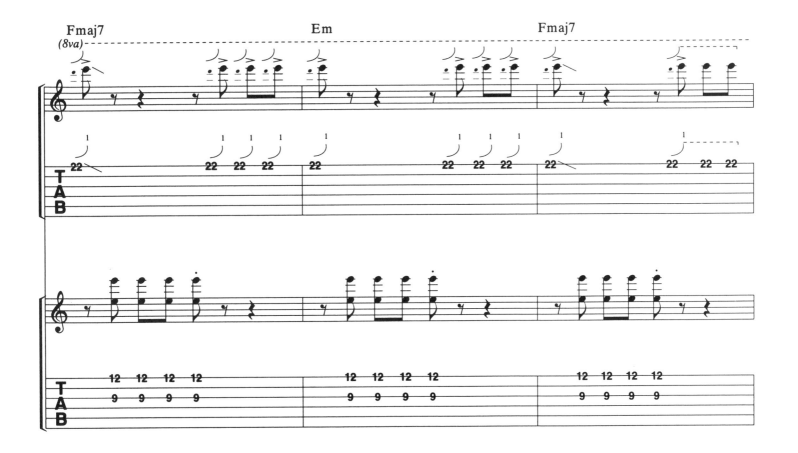

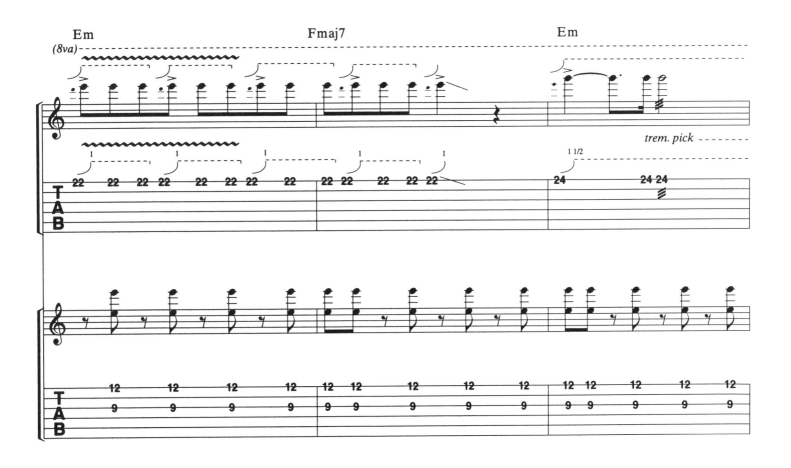

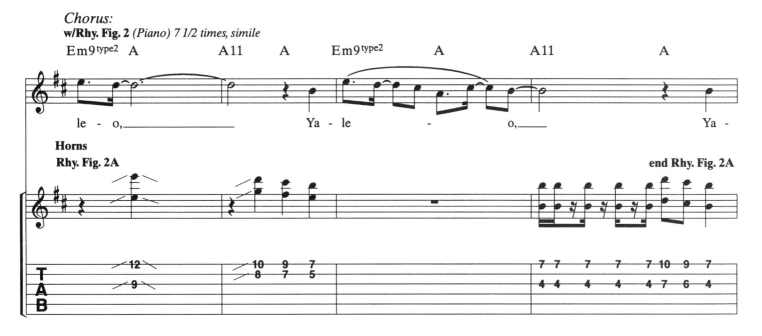

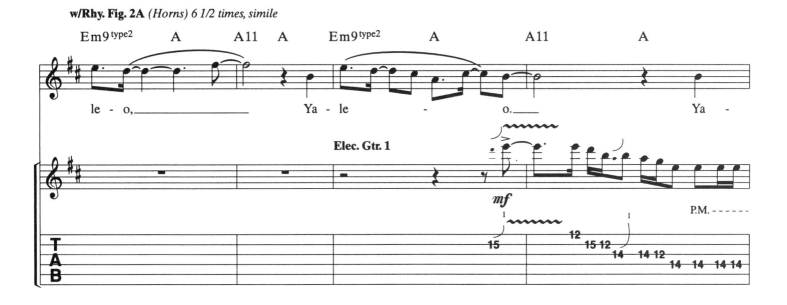

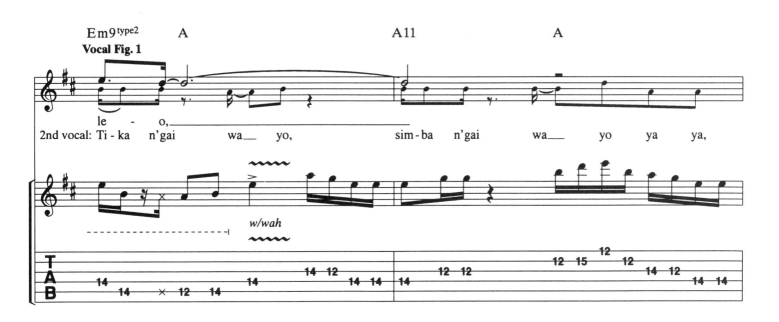

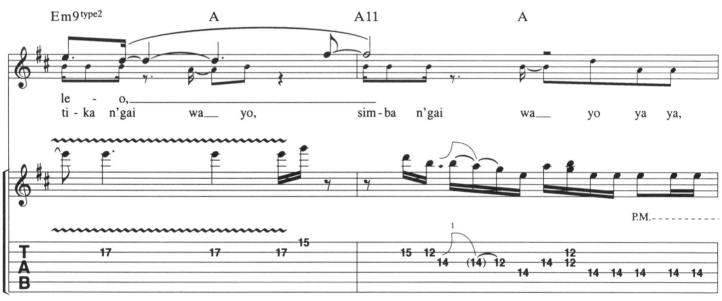

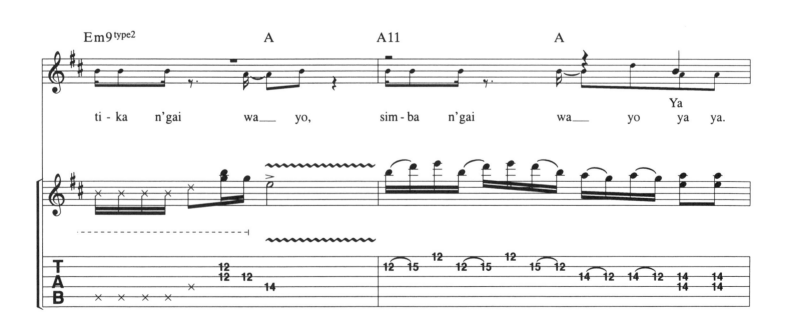

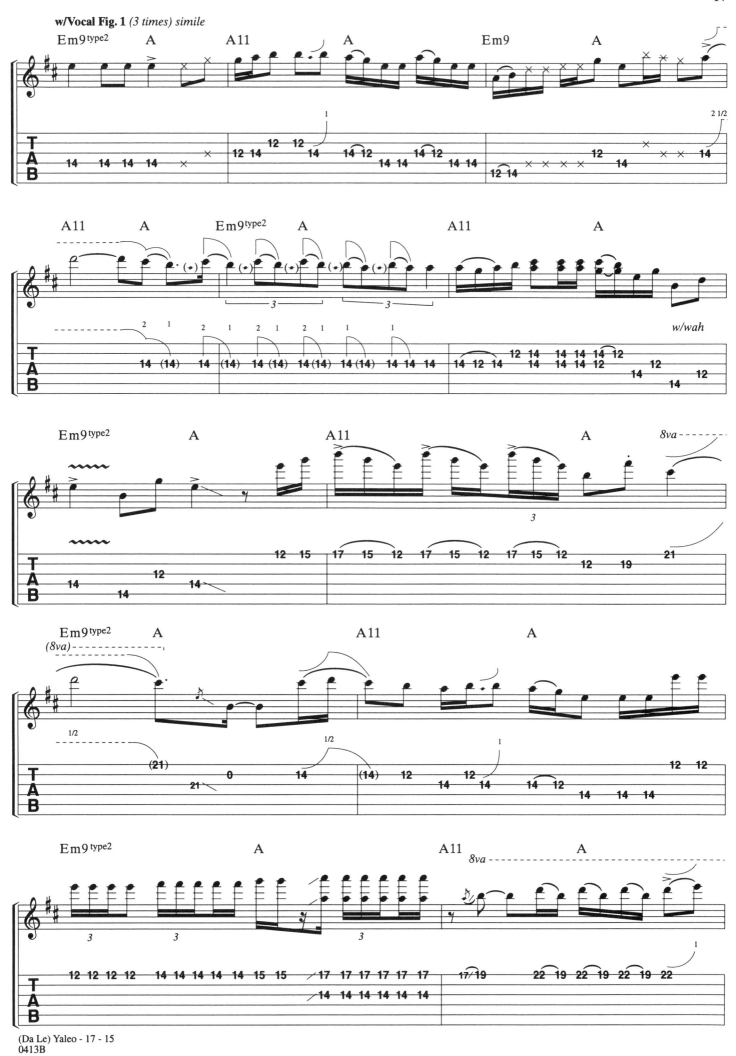

(Da Le) Yaleo - 17 - 15
0413B

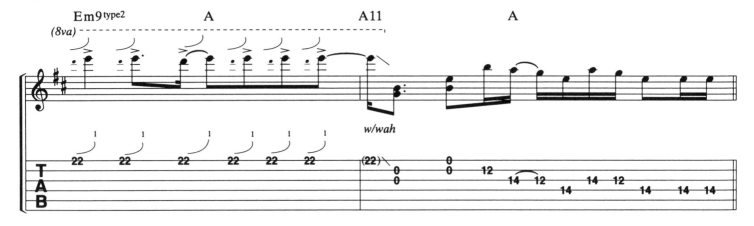

Outro:
w/Rhy. Figs. 2 *(Piano)* **& 2A** *(Horns) 4 1/4 times, simile*

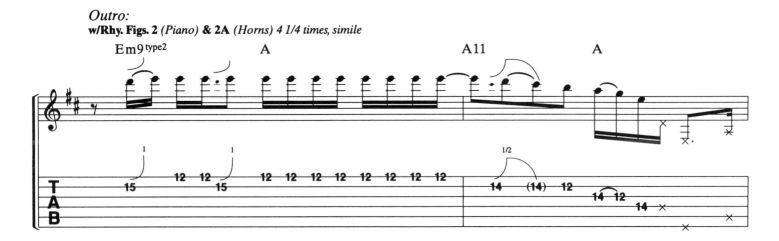

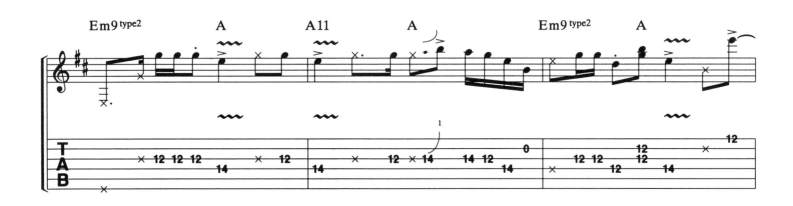

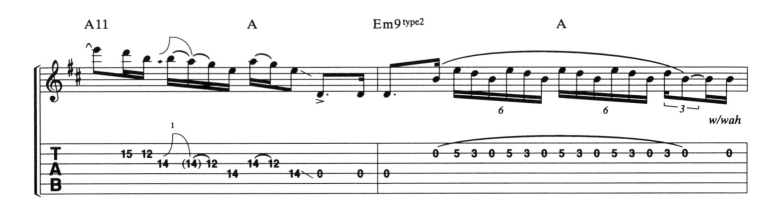

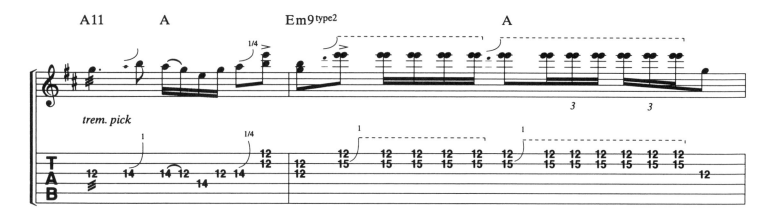

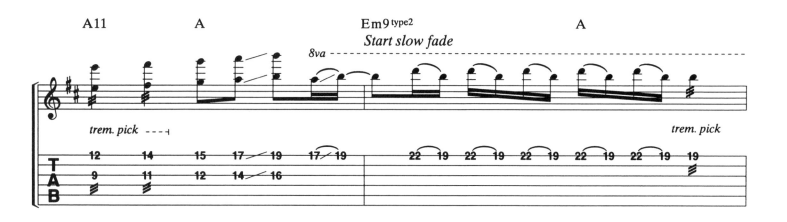

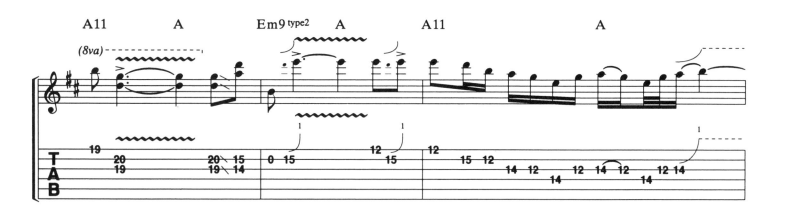

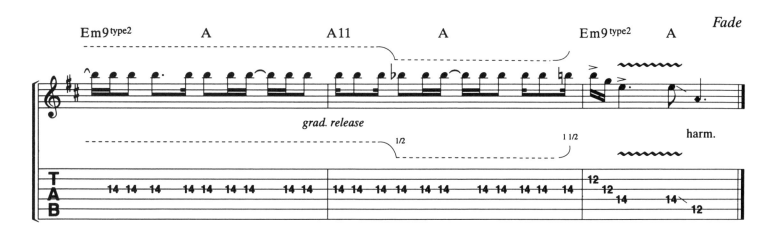

(Da Le) Yaleo - 17 - 17
0413B

LOVE OF MY LIFE

**Words and Music by
CARLOS SANTANA and DAVE MATTHEWS**

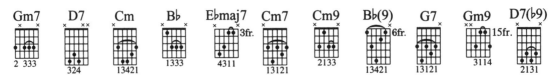

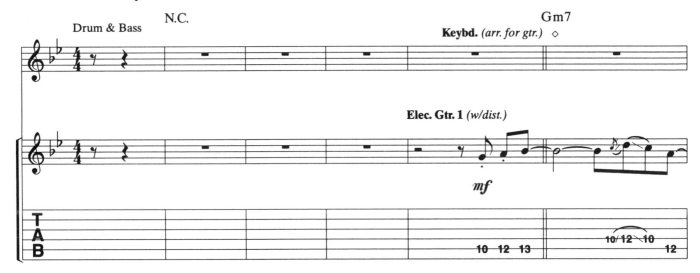

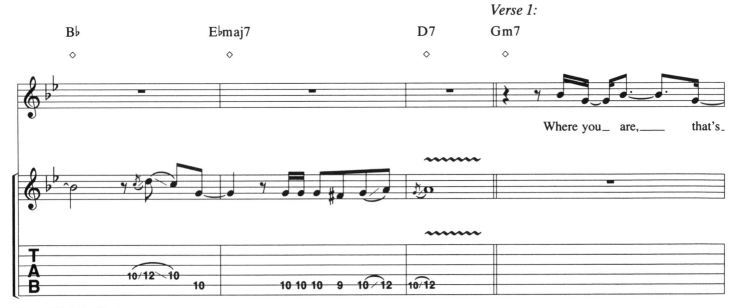

Love of My Life - 14 - 1
0413B

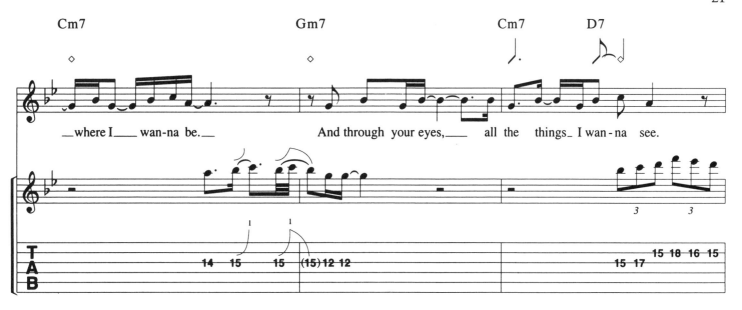

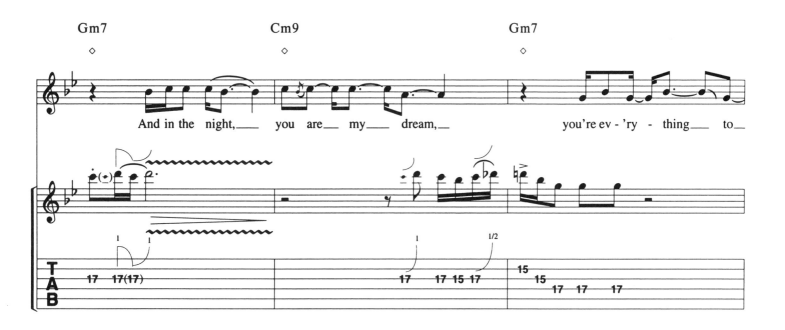

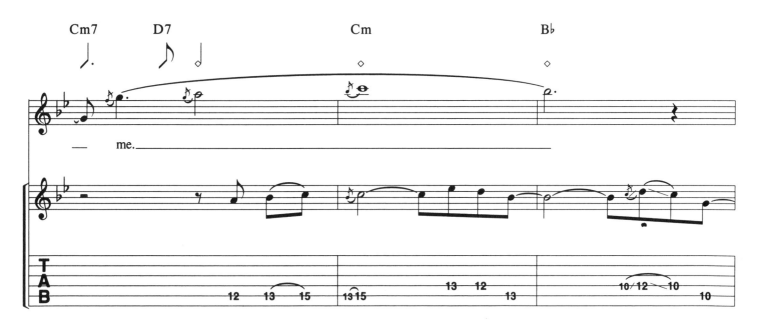

Chorus 1:

You're the love____

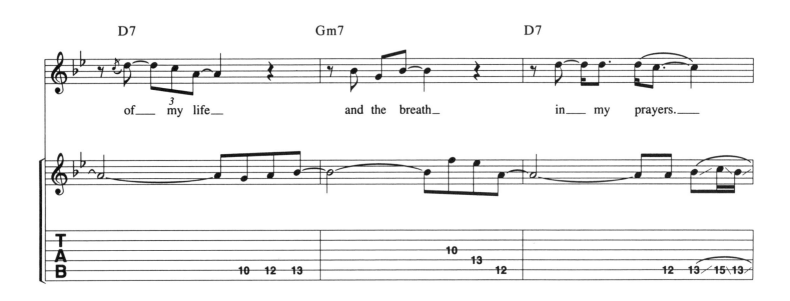

of____ my life____ and the breath____ in____ my prayers.____

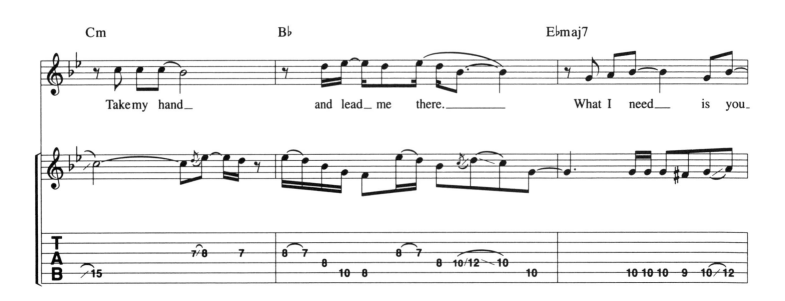

Take me my hand____ and lead____ me there._____ What I need____ is you____

Verse 2:

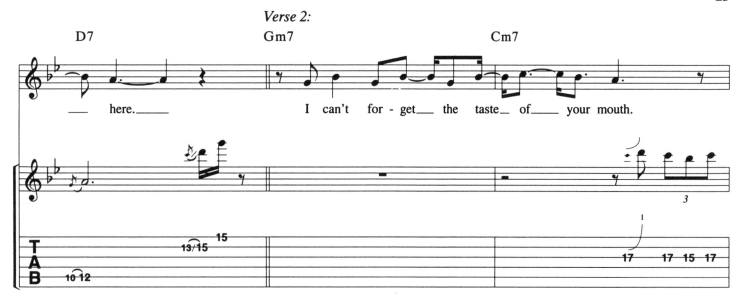

here._____ I can't for-get___ the taste_ of____ your mouth.

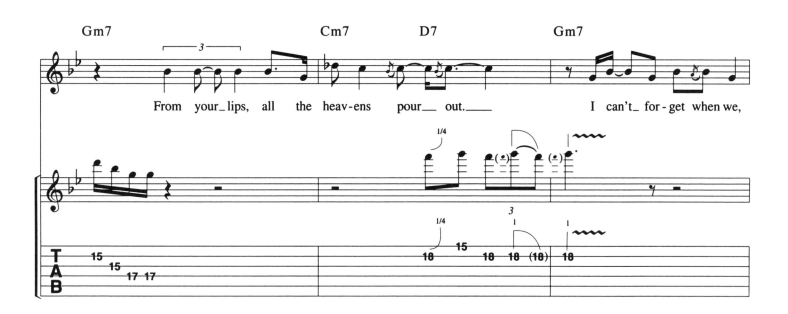

From your_lips, all the heav-ens pour_ out.____ I can't_ for-get when we,

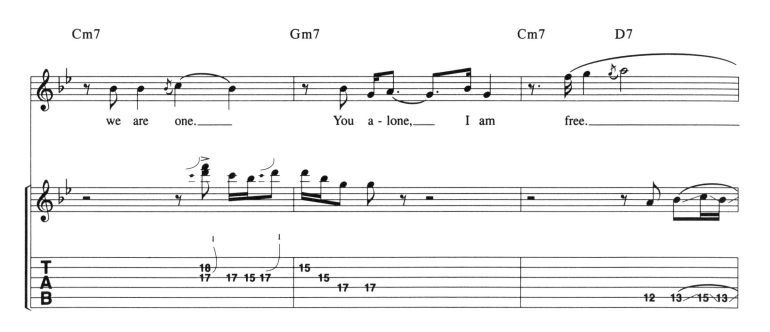

we are one.____ You a-lone,____ I am free.____

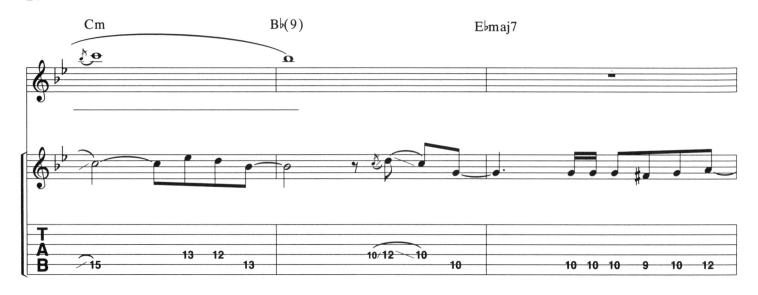

Chorus 2:

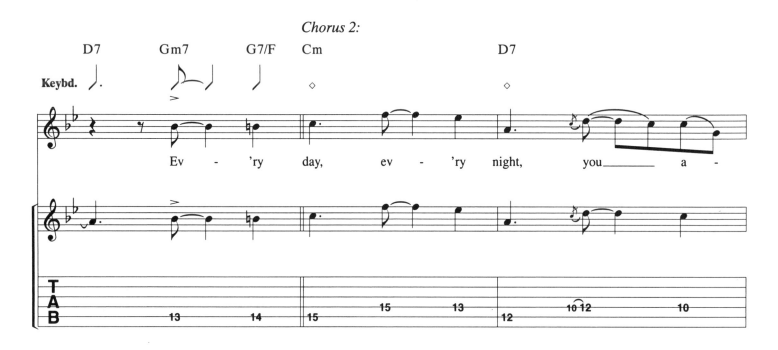

Ev - 'ry day, ev - 'ry night, you_____ a -

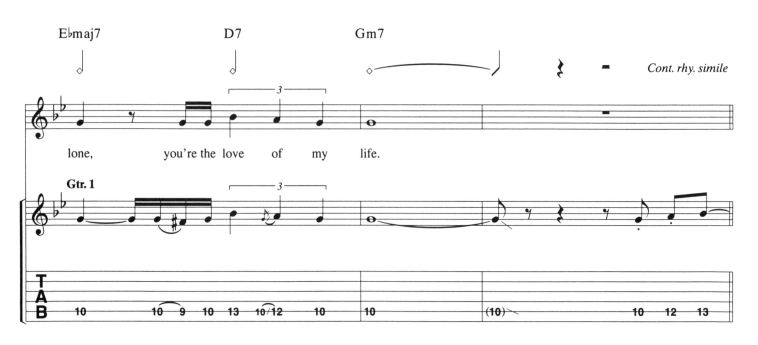

lone, you're the love of my life.

26

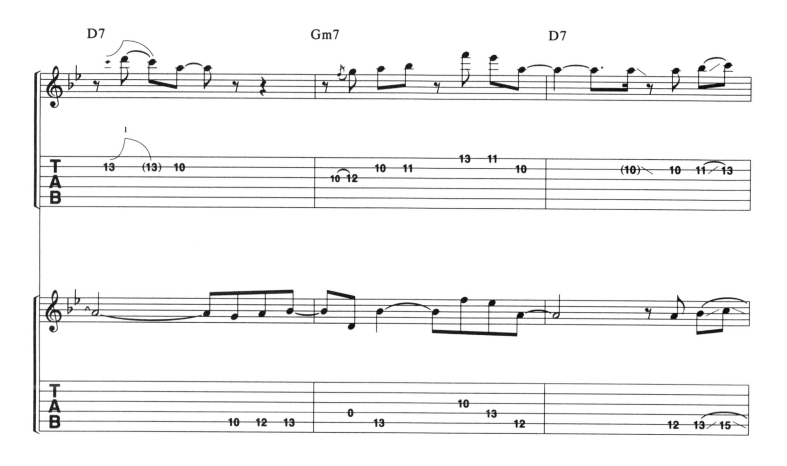

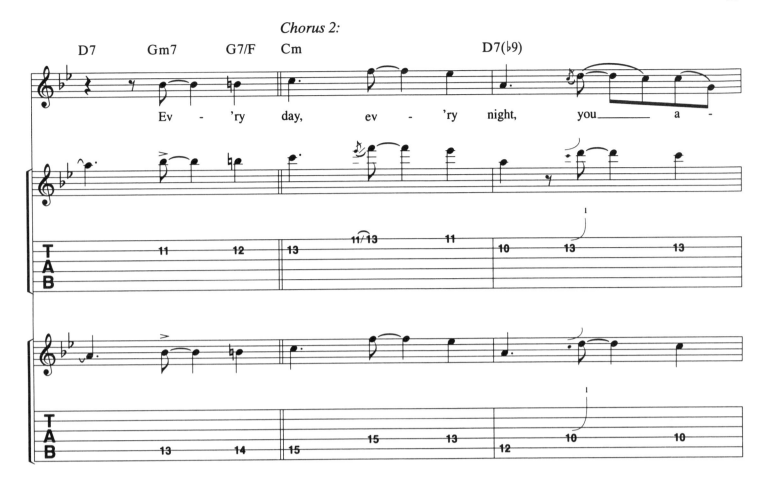

Love of My Life - 14 - 8
0413B

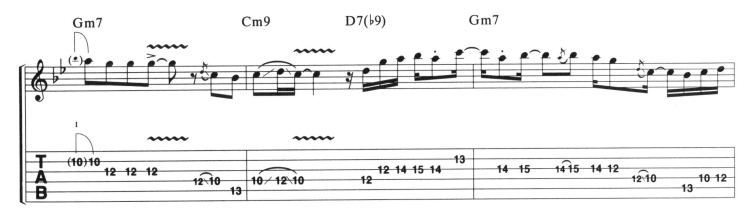

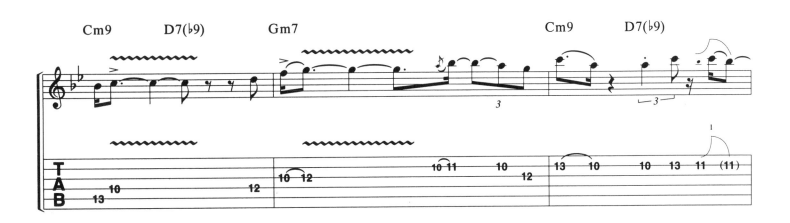

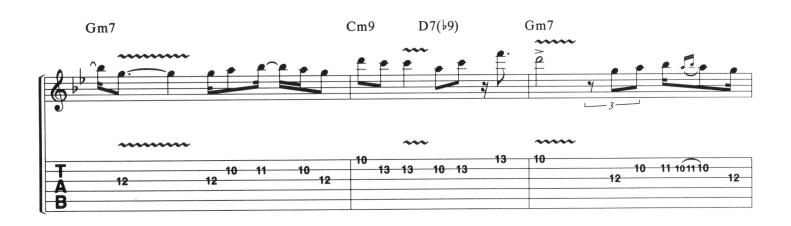

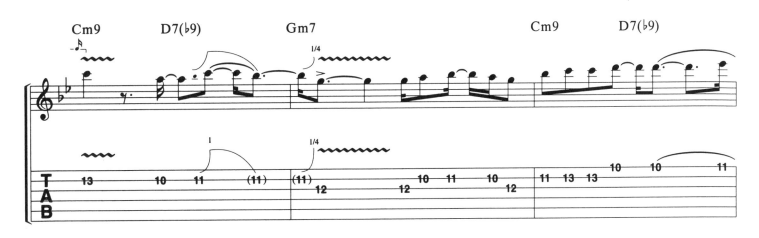

30

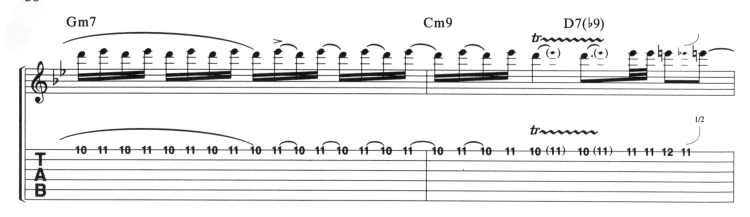

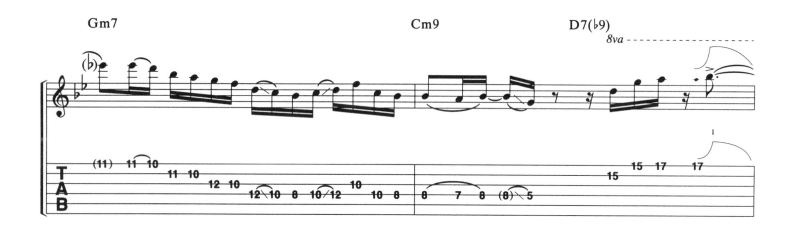

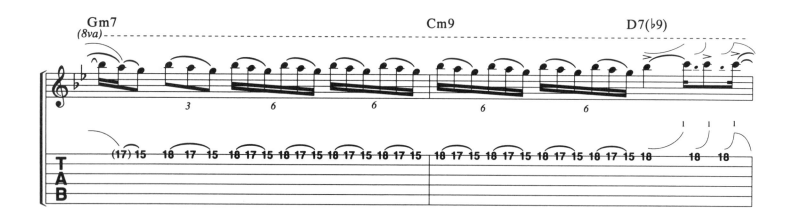

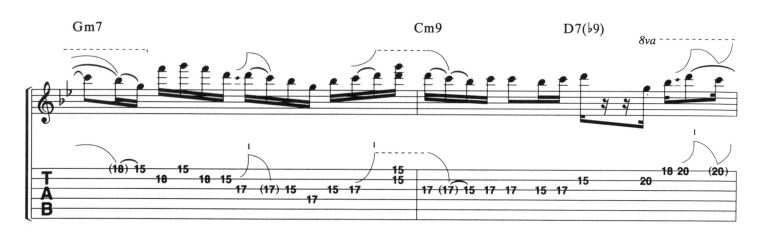

Love of My Life - 14 - 11
0413B

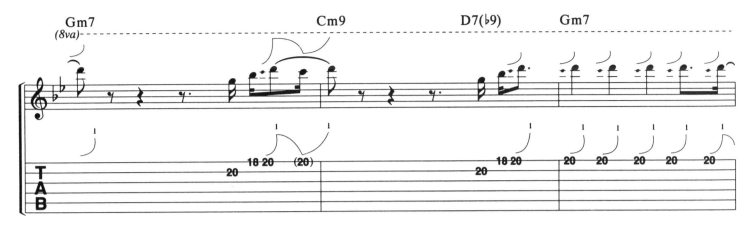

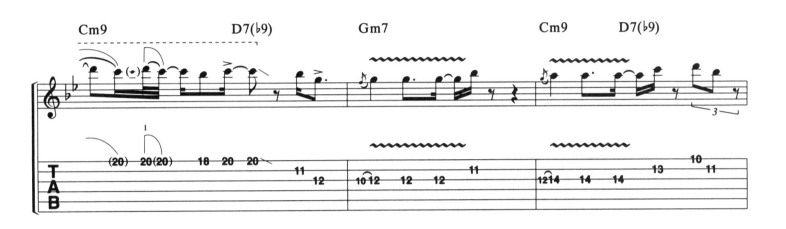

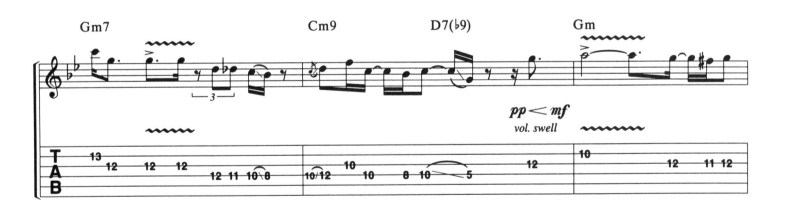

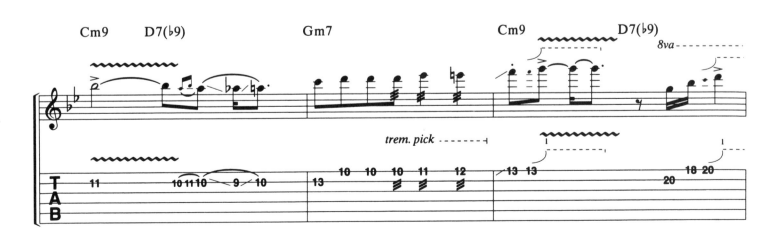

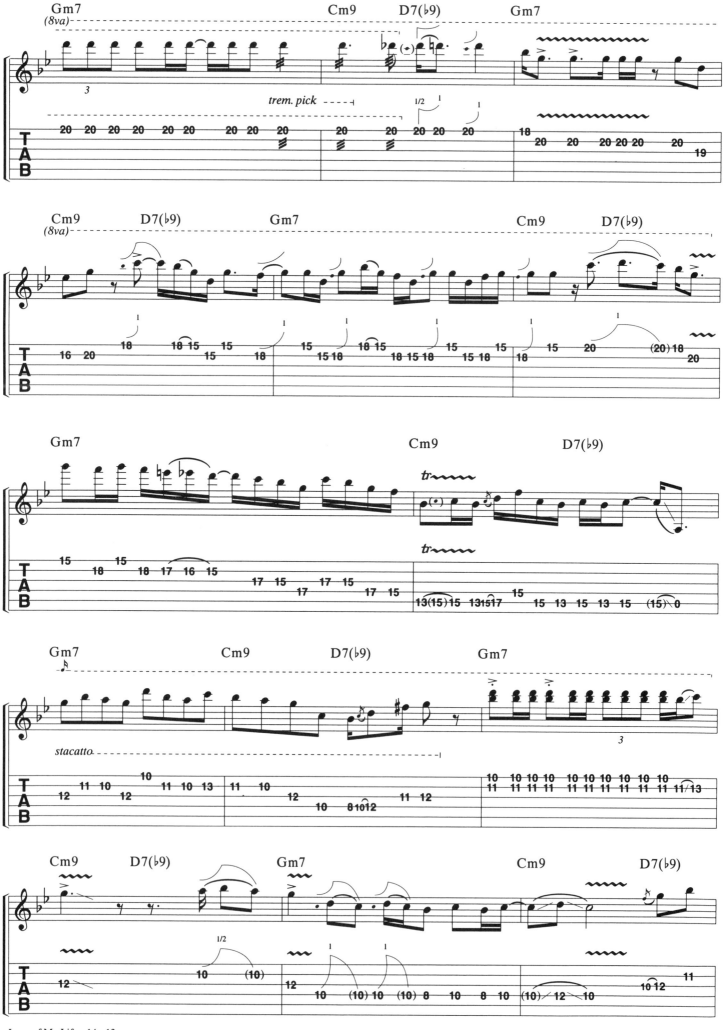

PUT YOUR LIGHTS ON

Words and Music by
ERIK SCHRODY

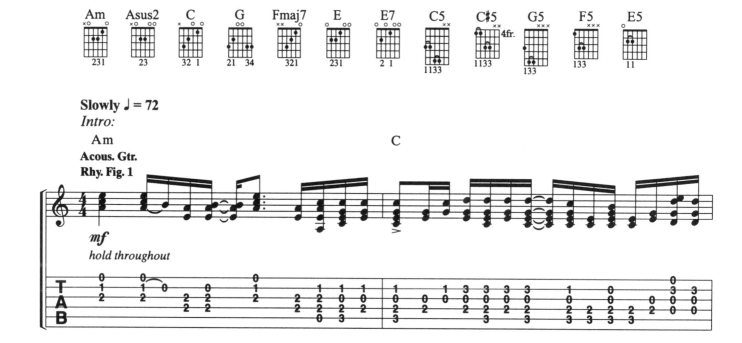

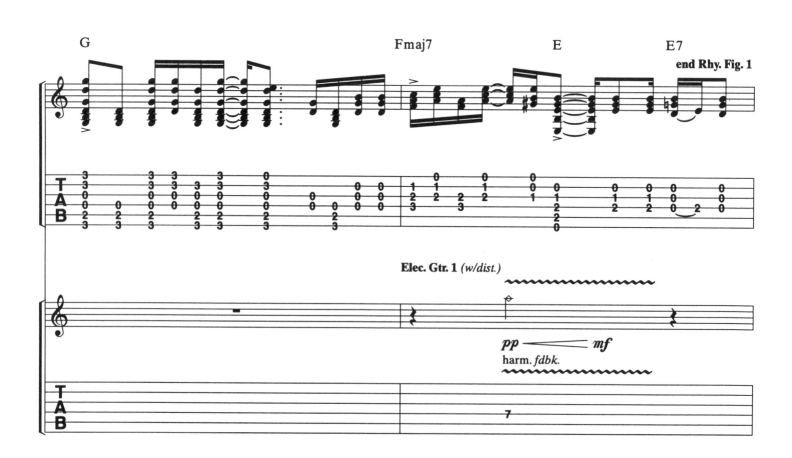

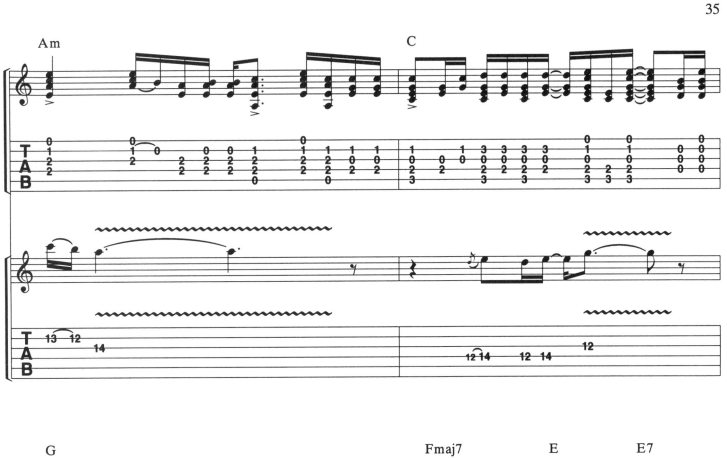

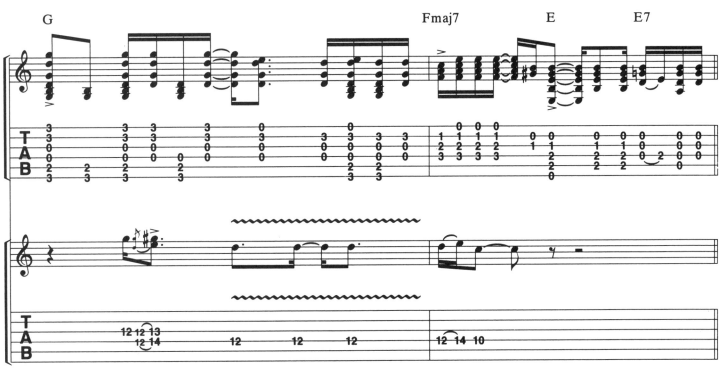

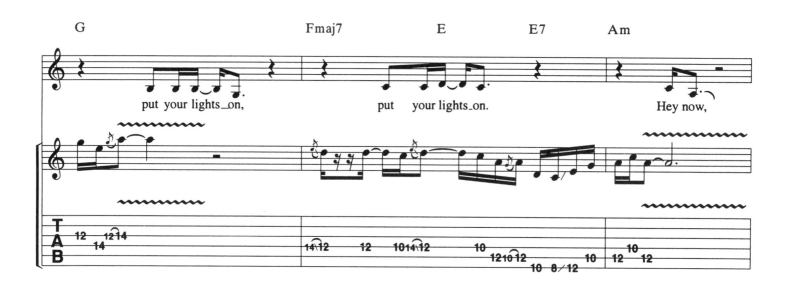

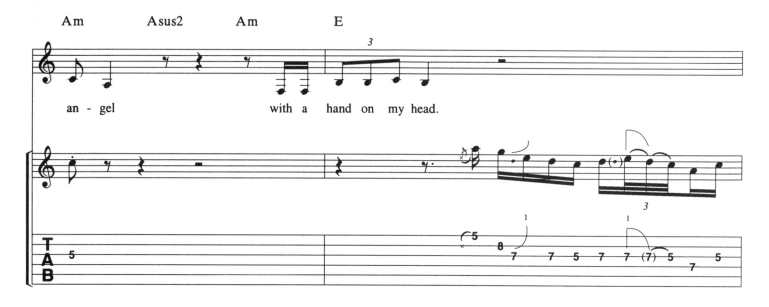

an - gel   with a hand on my head.

She say I got noth-ing to fear.___   There's a

Verse 2:
w/Rhy. Fig. 3 *(Acous. Gtr. 1) 4 times, simile*

dark - ness   liv-ing deep in my soul,___

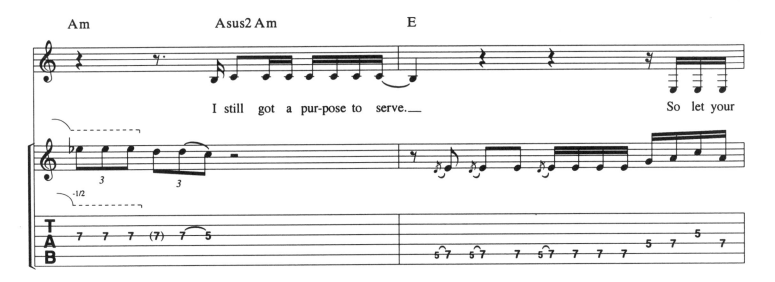

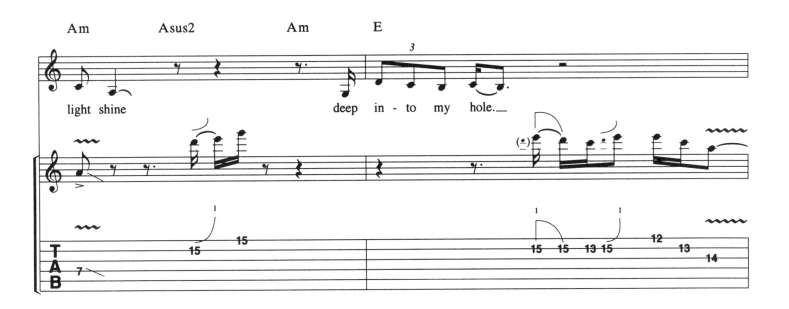

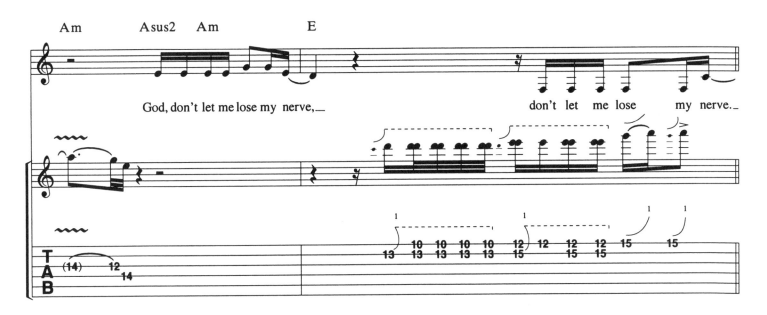

Guitar Solo:

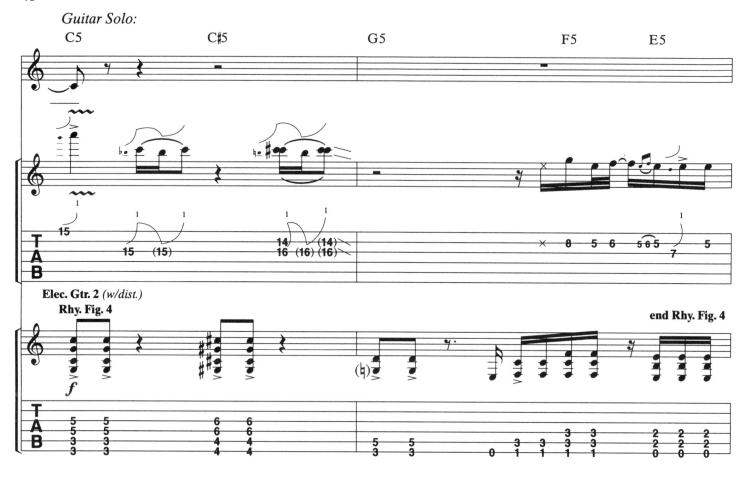

Elec. Gtr. 2 *(w/dist.)*

w/Rhy. Fig. 4 *(Elec. Gtr. 2) 3 times, simile*

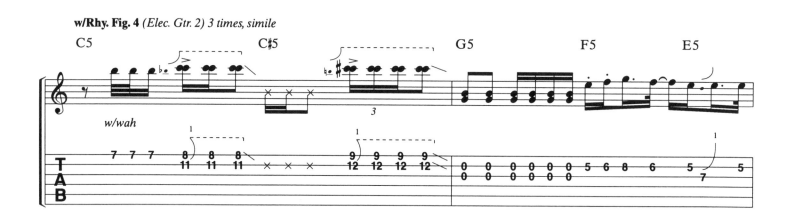

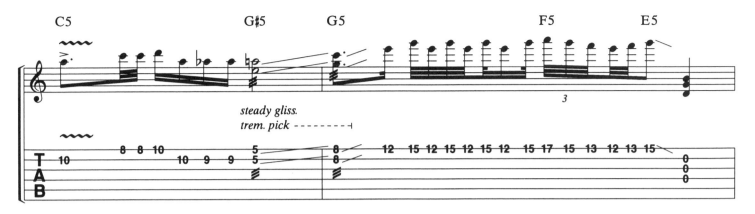

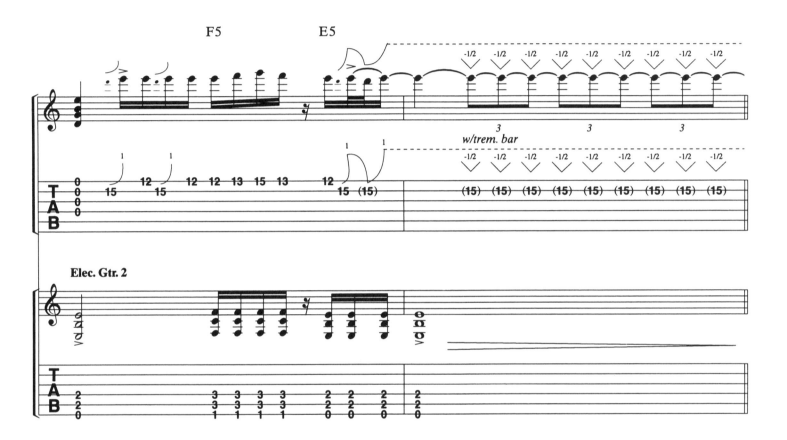

*Echo repeats in parenthesis.

Chorus:
w/Rhy. Fig. 2 (Acous. Gtr.) 2 times, simile

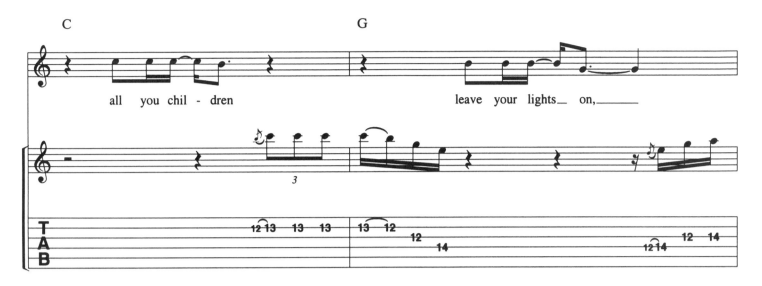

Verse 3:
w/Rhy. Fig. 3 *(Acous. Gtr.) 4 times, simile*

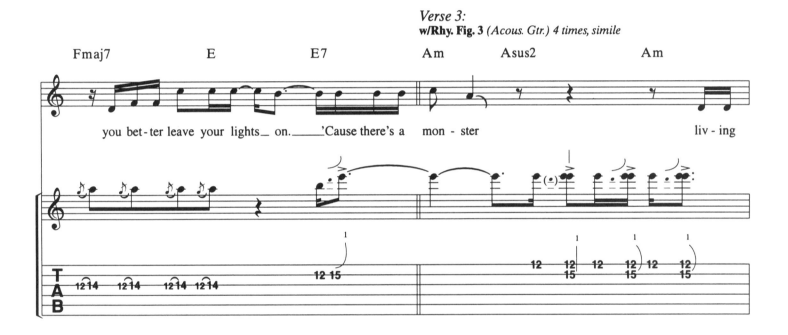

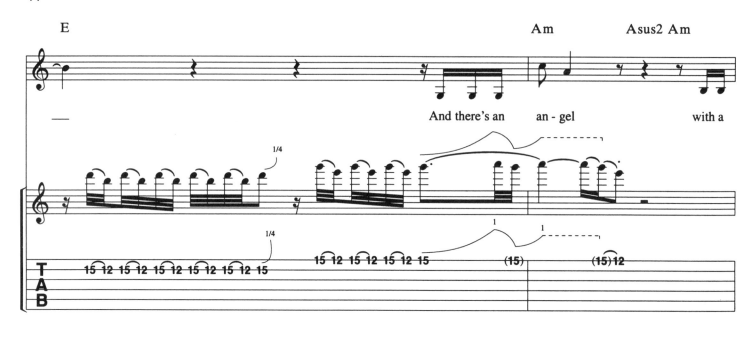

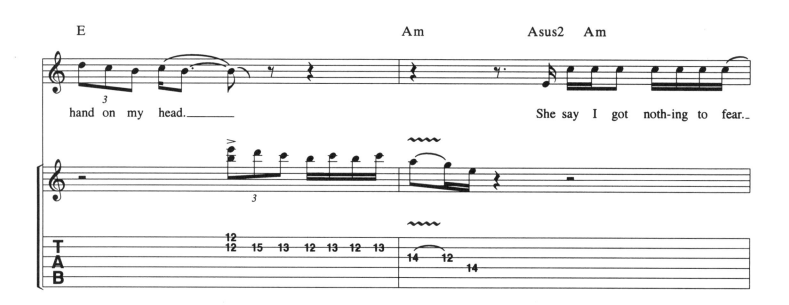

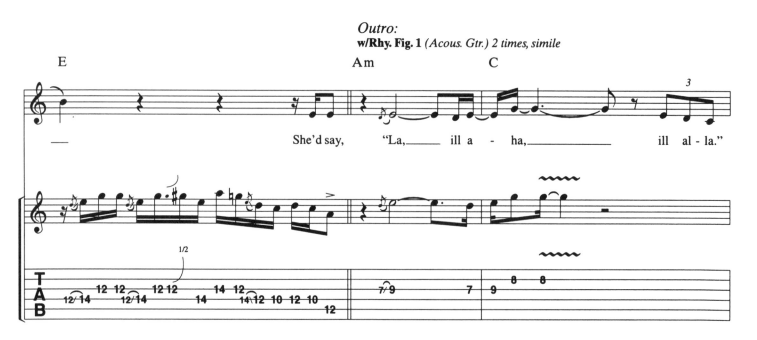

AFRICA BAMBA

**Words and Music by
ISMALIA TOURE, S. TIDIANE TOURE,
CARLOS SANTANA and KARL PERAZZO**

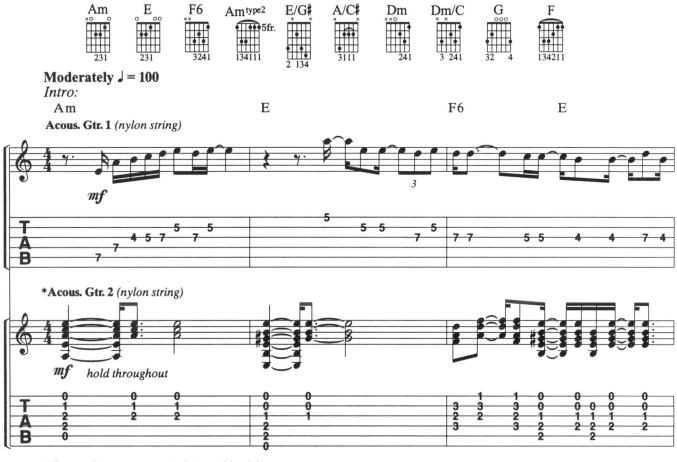

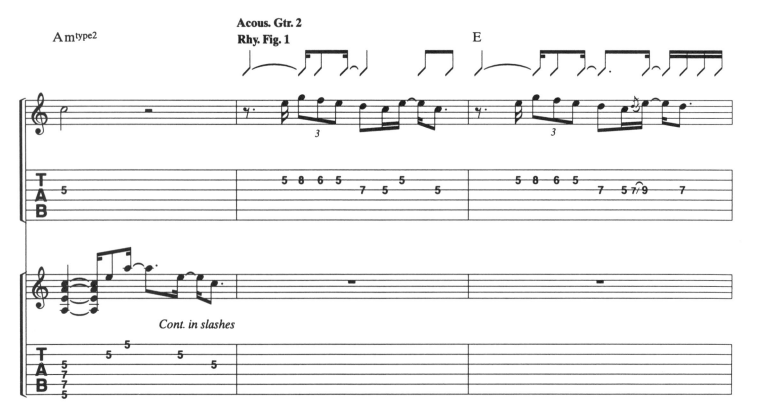

Africa Bamba - 12 - 1
0413B

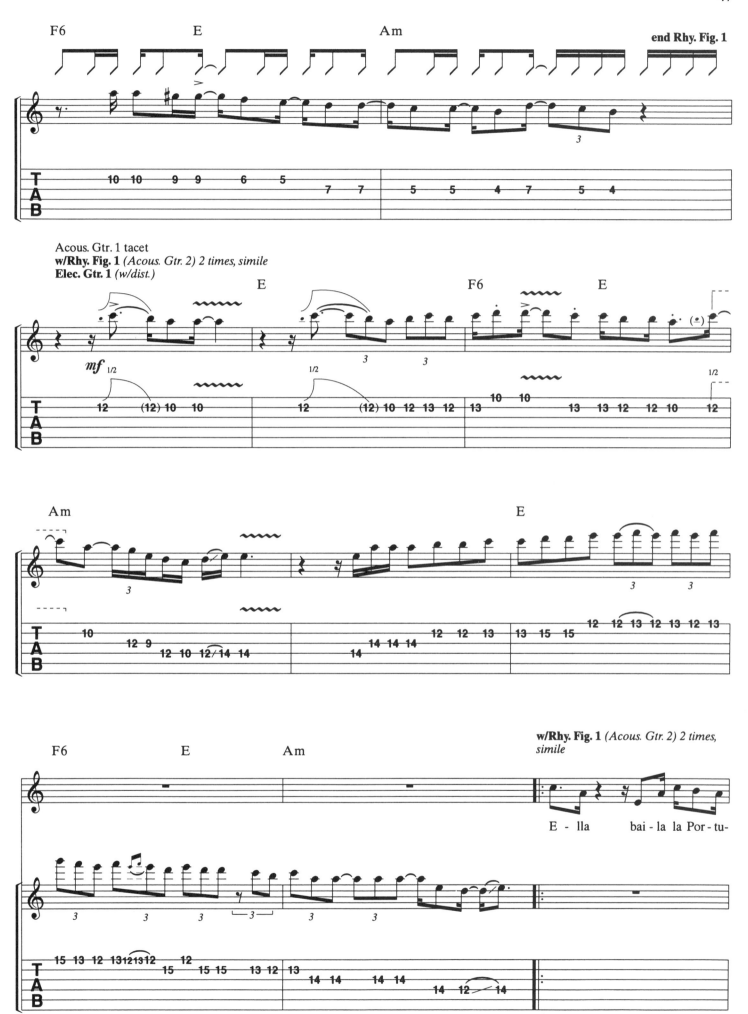

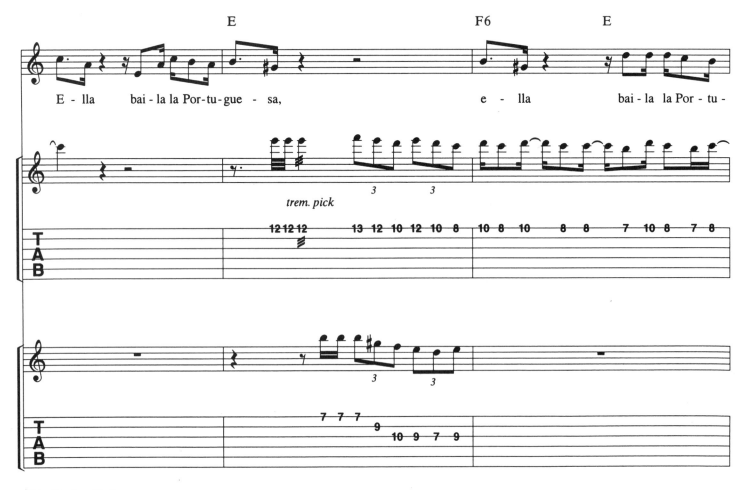

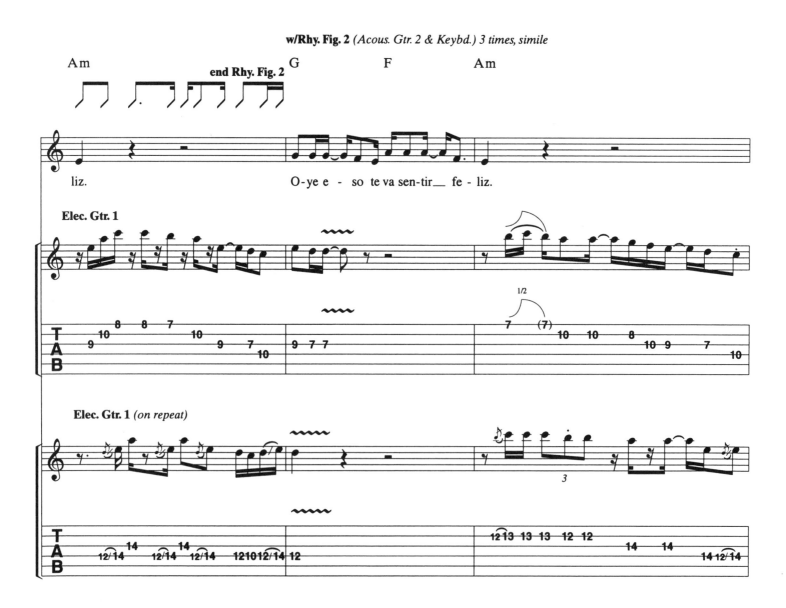

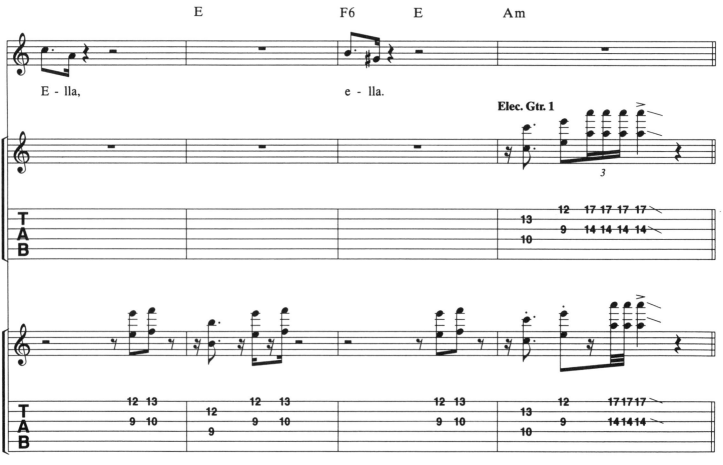

Guitar Solo:
w/Rhy. Fig. 2 *(Acous. Gtr. 2 & Keybd.) 7 1/2 times, simile*

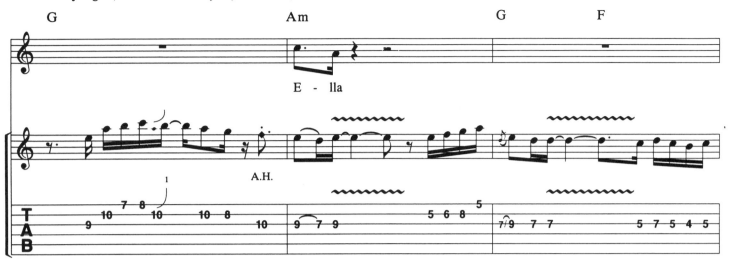

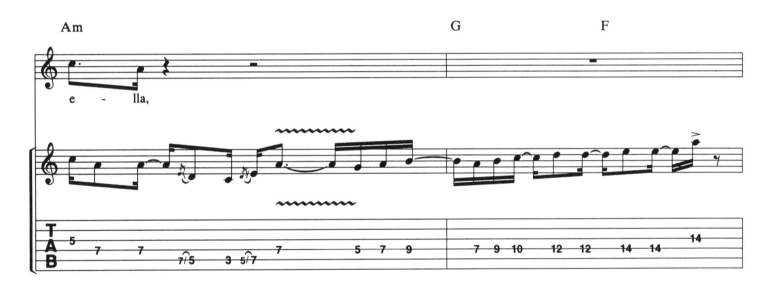

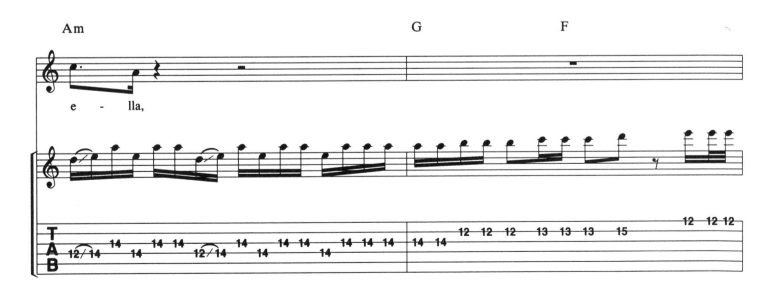

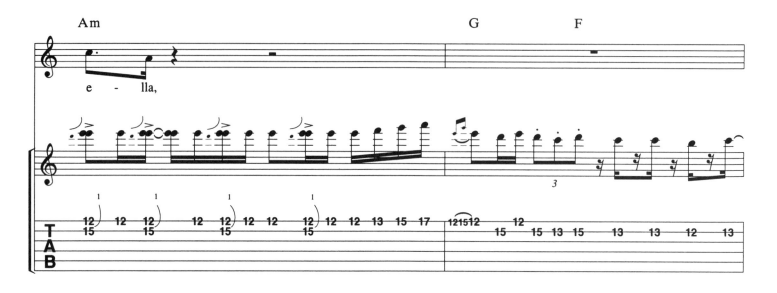

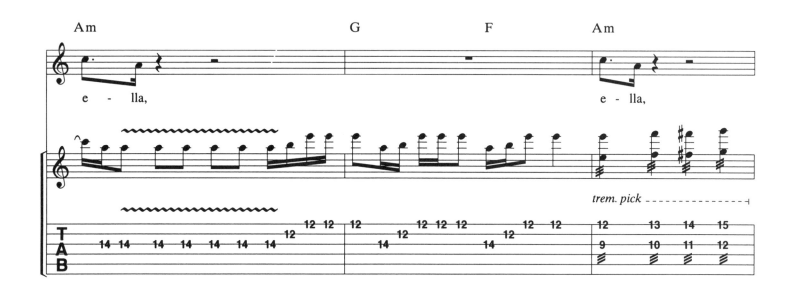

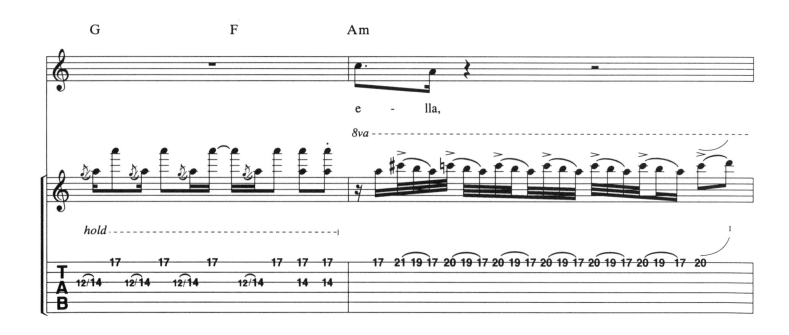

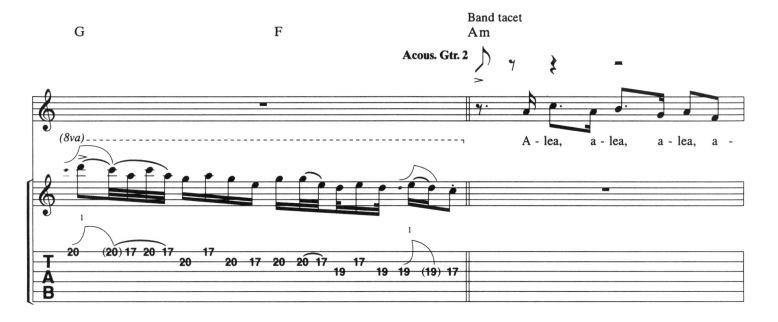

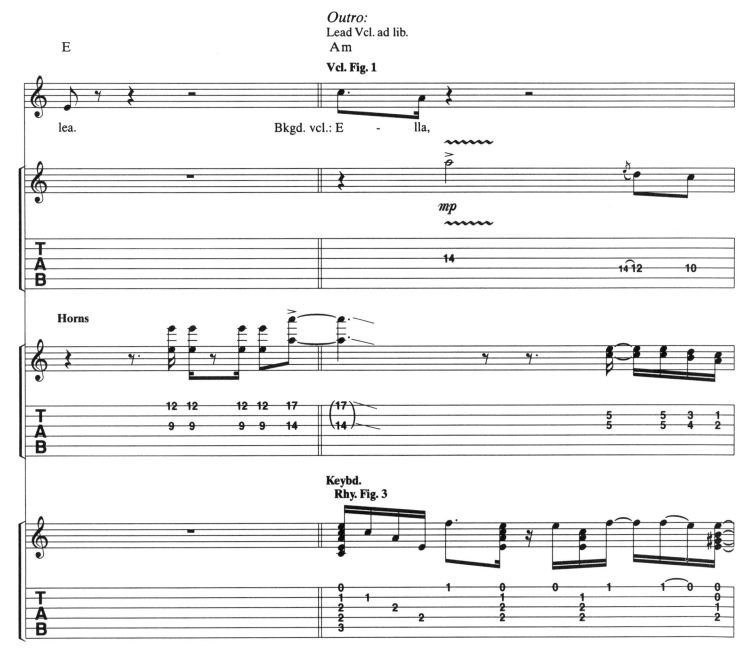

Africa Bamba - 12 - 10
0413B

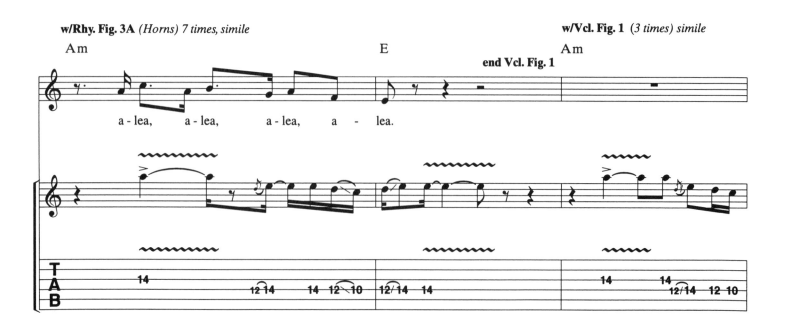

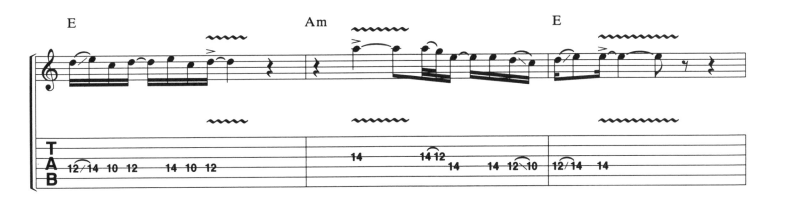

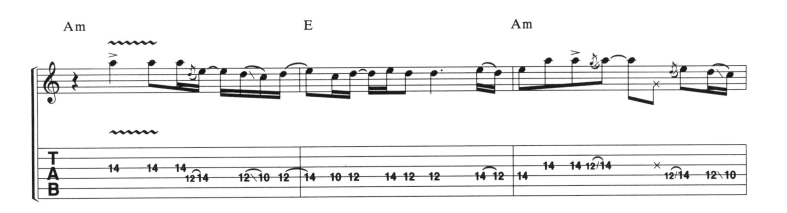

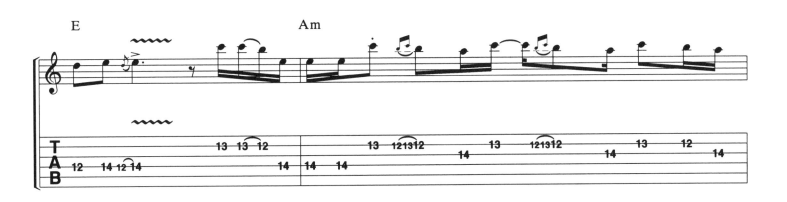

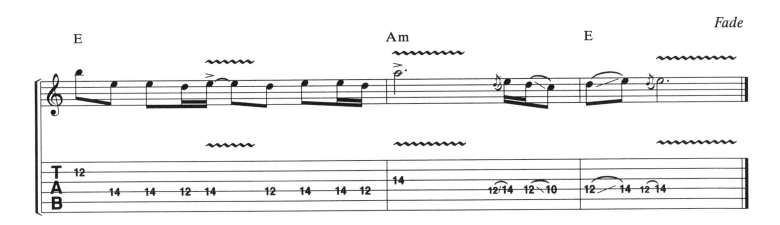

SMOOTH

Music and Lyrics by
ITAAL SHUR and ROB THOMAS

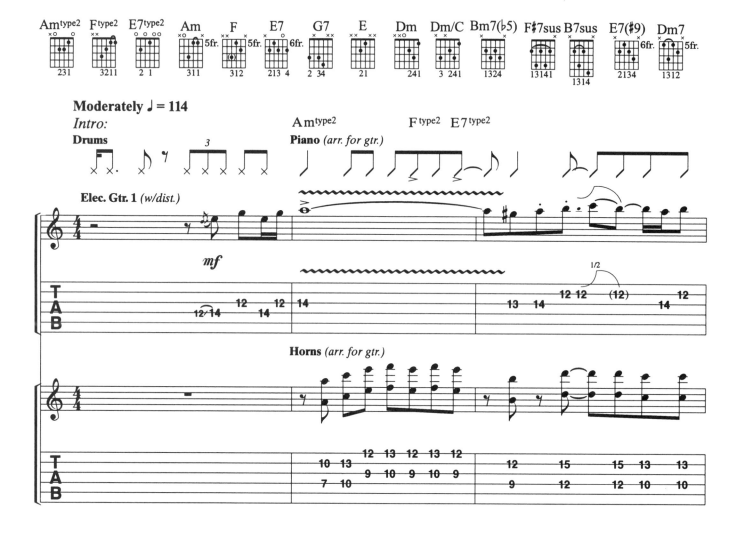

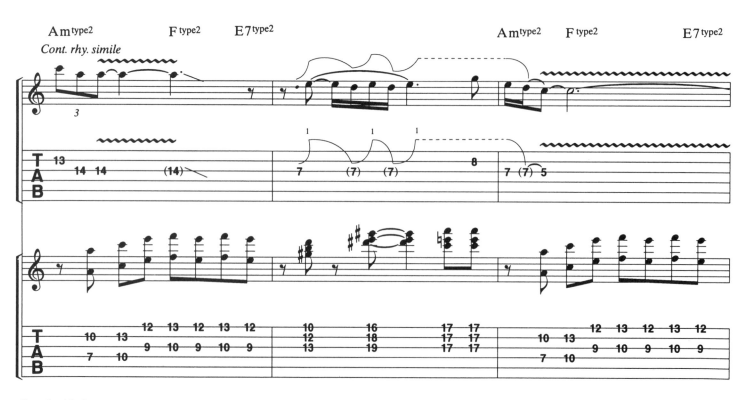

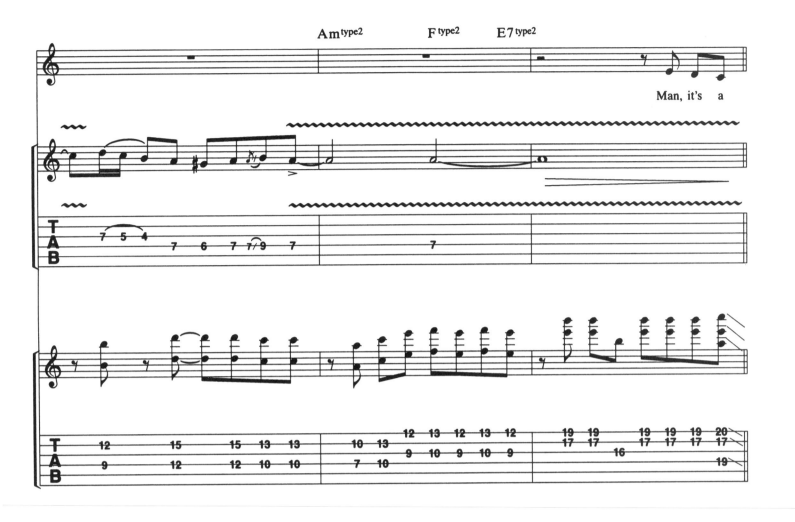

Verse 1:

Well, I hear your whis-per and the words   melt ev - 'ry - one._____ But you stay____ so____

cool.____   My   Mu - ñe - qui - ta,

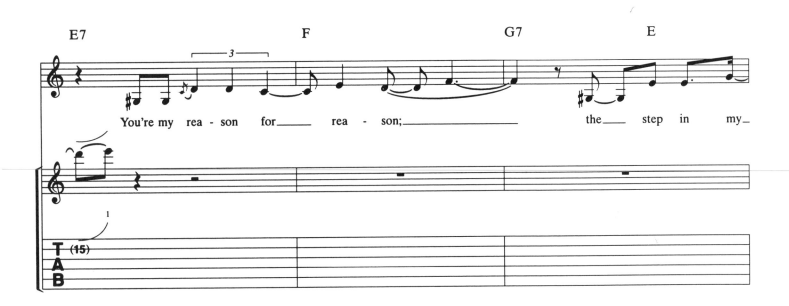

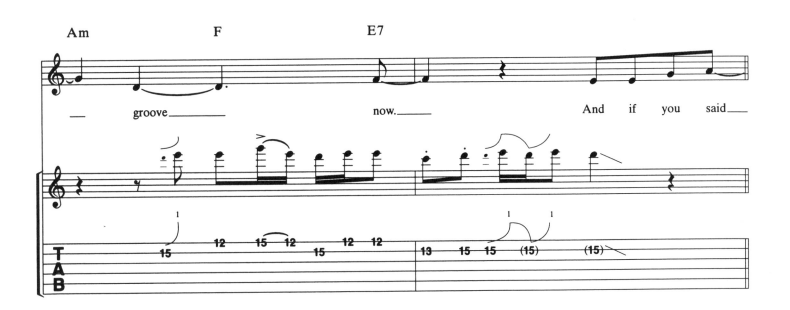

𝄋 *Pre-chorus:*

this life ain't good e - nough,__ I would give__ my world to

lift you up.__ I could change__ my life to bet - ter suit__ your__ mood.__

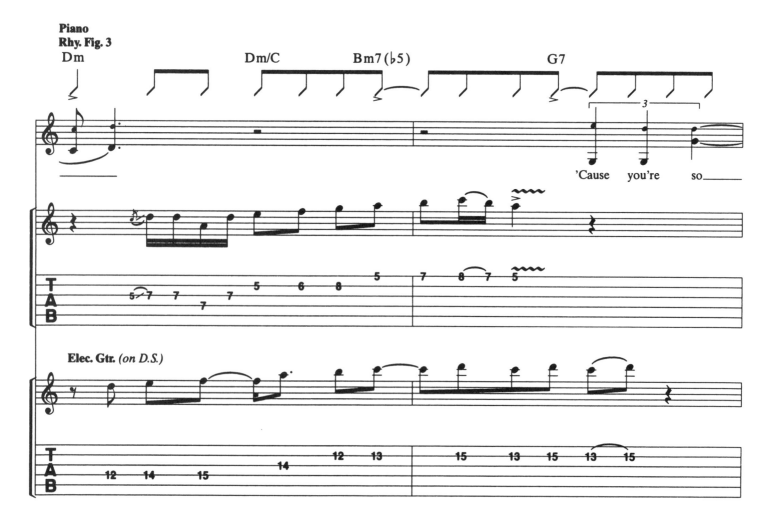

'Cause you're so__

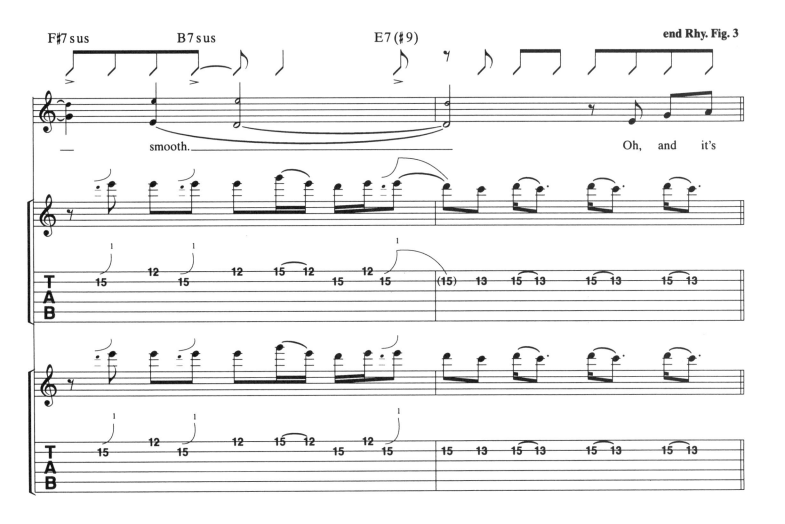

⅀⅀ *Chorus:*

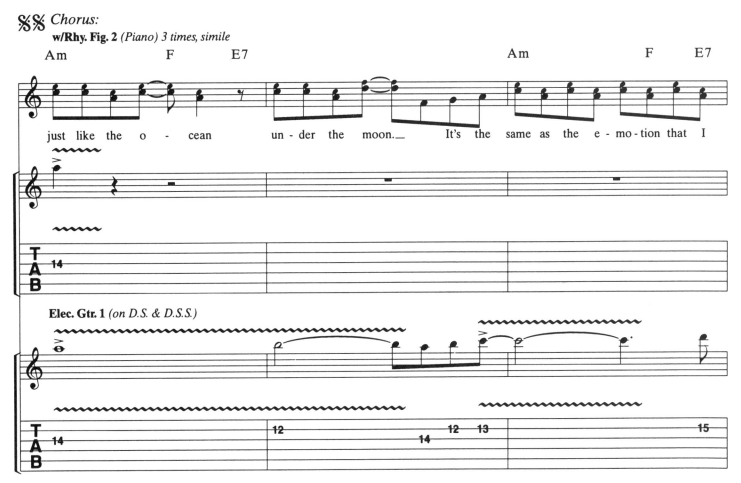

get from you.___ You got the kind of lov - ing that can be so smooth,_ yeah.

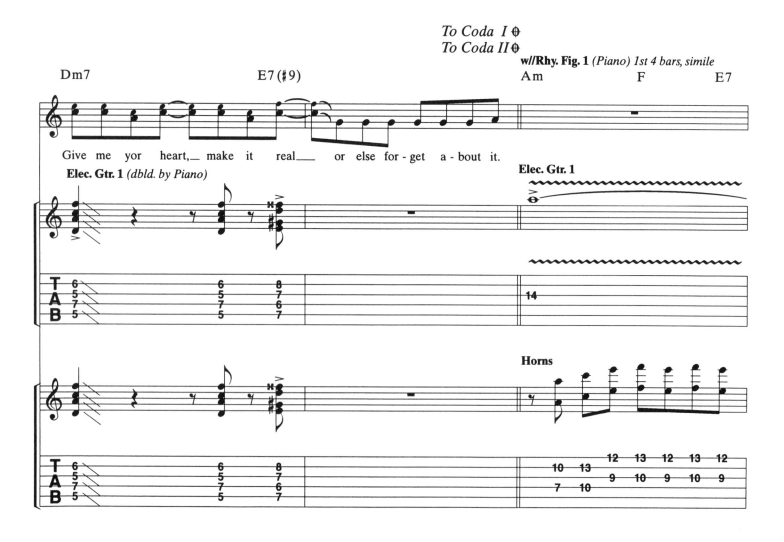

To Coda I ⊕
To Coda II ⊕

w//Rhy. **Fig. 1** *(Piano) 1st 4 bars, simile*

Give me yor heart,_ make it real___ or else for-get a-bout it.

Elec. Gtr. 1 *(dbld. by Piano)*

Elec. Gtr. 1

Horns

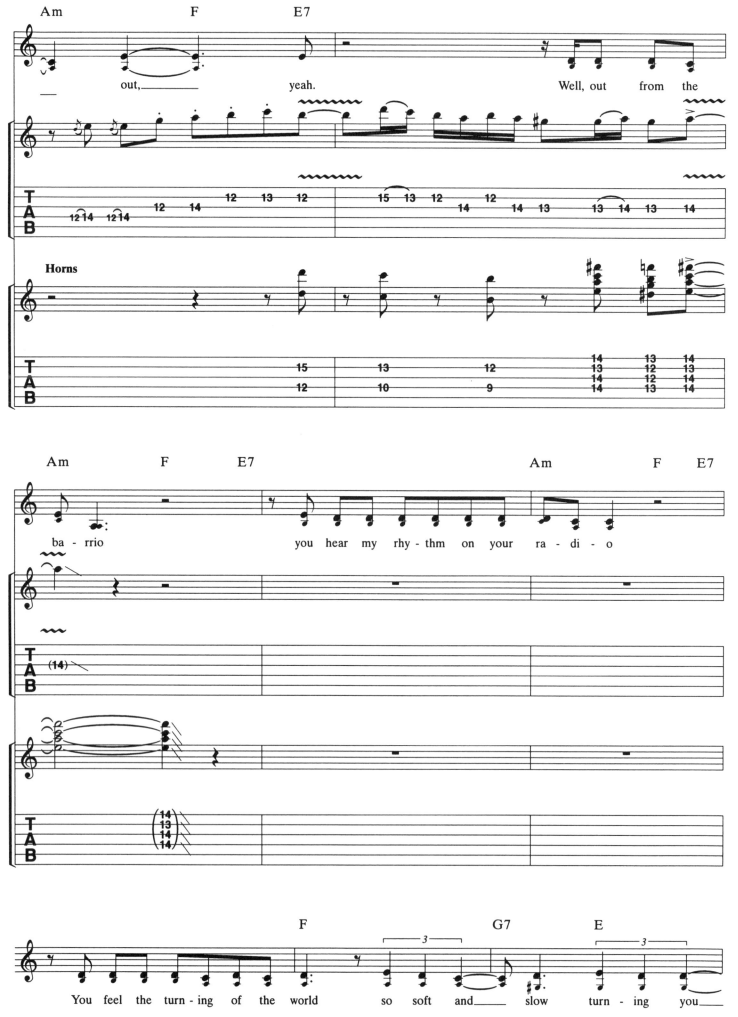

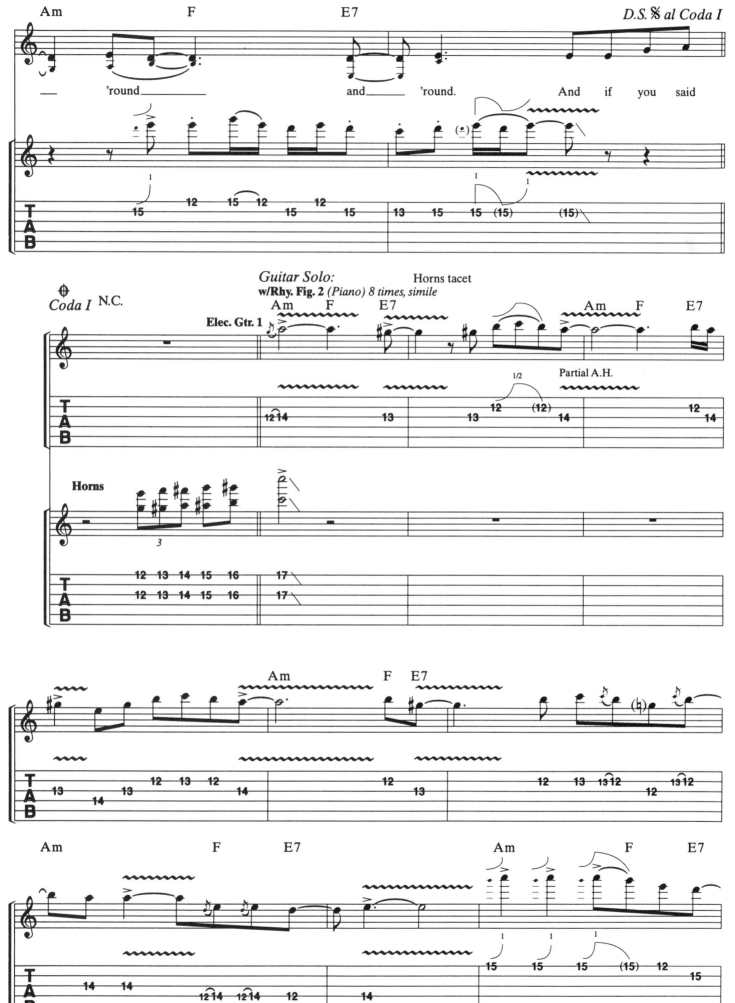

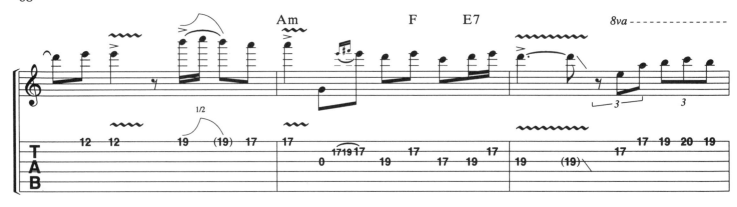

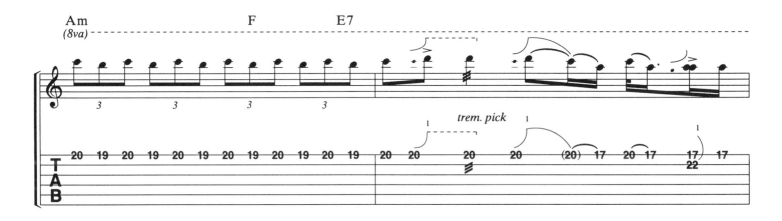

w/Rhy. Fig. 3 *(Piano) simile*

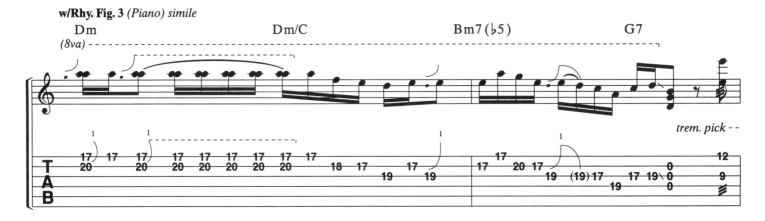

D.S.S. 𝄌𝄌 al Coda II

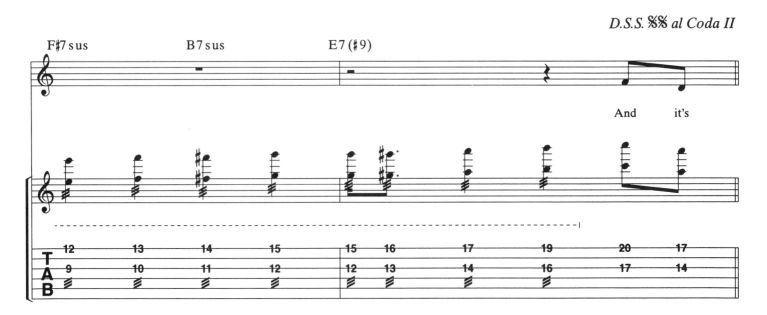

Coda II

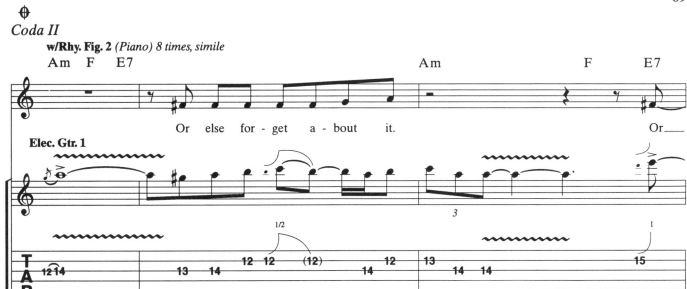

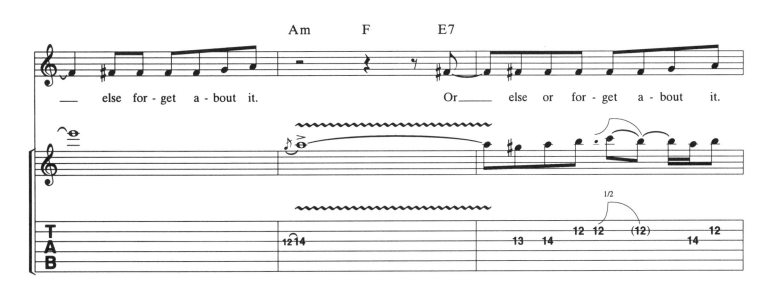

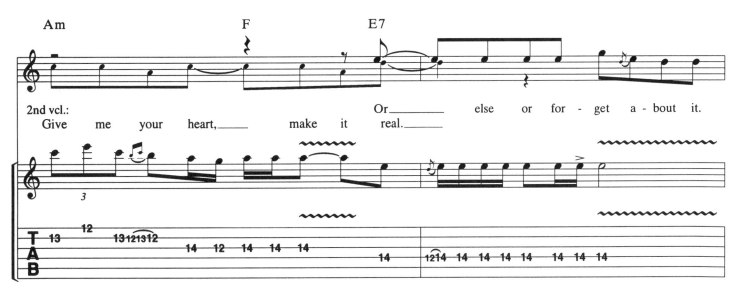

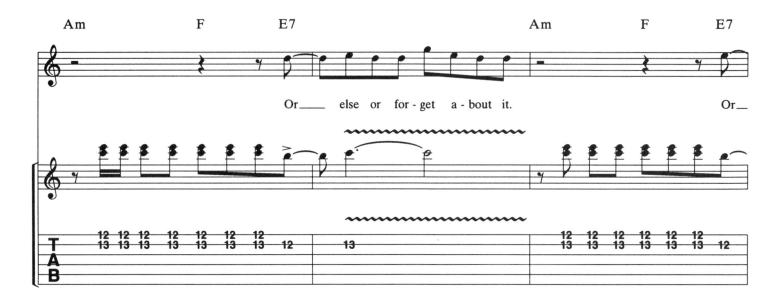

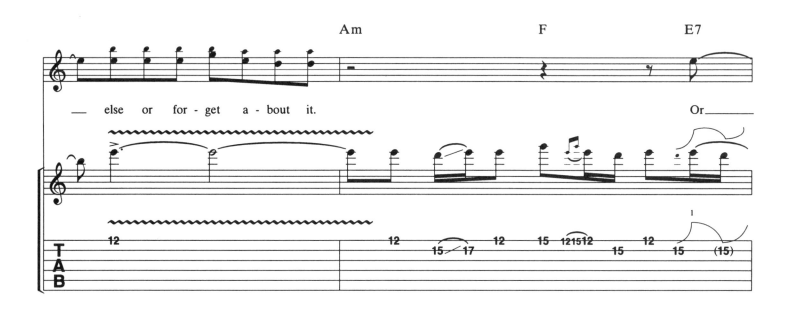

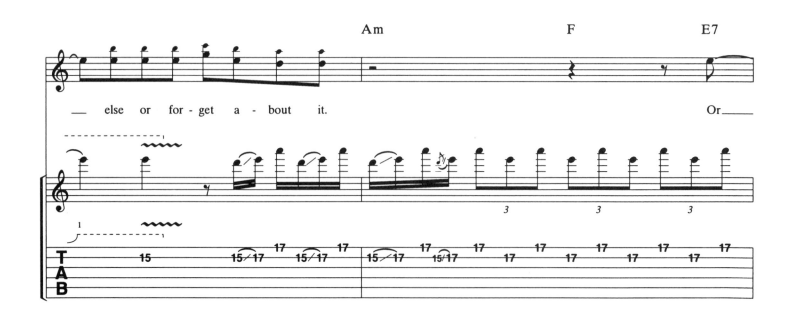

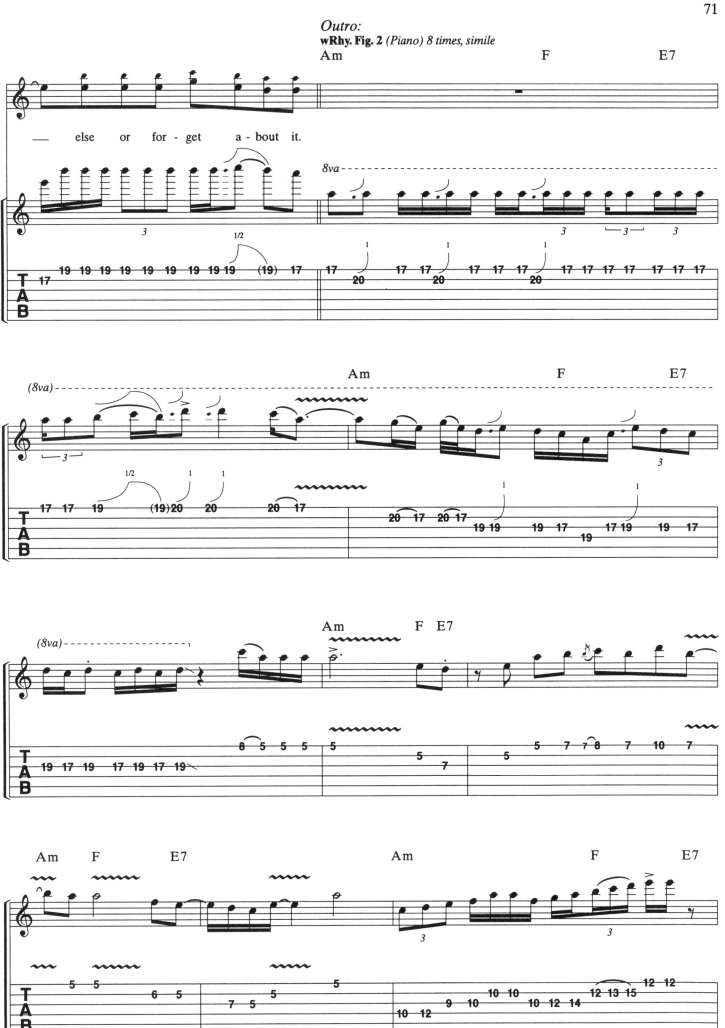

Smooth - 15 - 14
0413B

Slow Fade

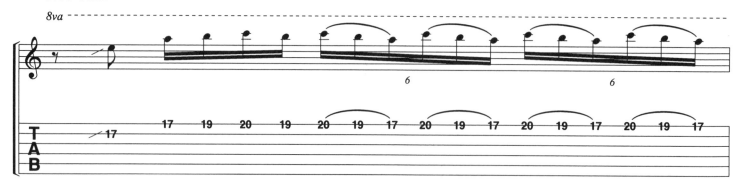

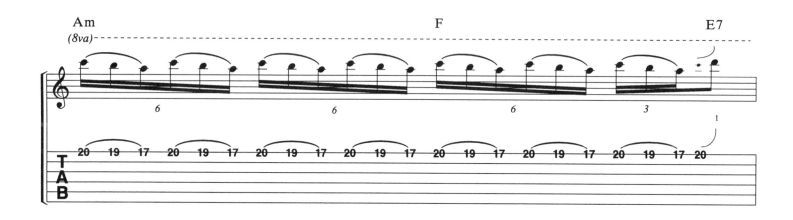

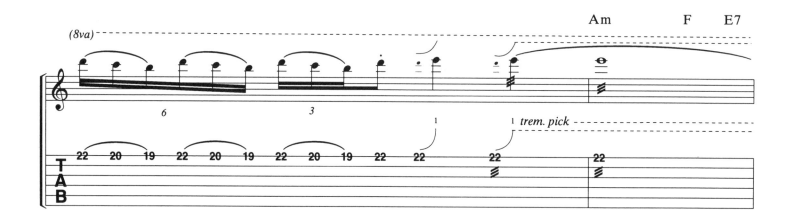

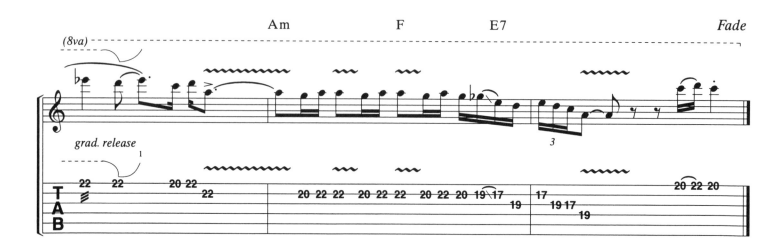

DO YOU LIKE THE WAY

Words and Music by
LAURYN HILL

end Vocal Fig. 1

F#m7

way? Ah._____ Do you like_the way, like the way?_ Ah._____

Verse 1:
w/Rhy. Figs. 1 *(Horns)* **& 1A** *(Elec. Gtr. 2) simile*

Em7 type3

Watch the mas - ter plan, the pas - tures span. Through the streets,

Acous. Gtr. 1 *(nylon string)*
Rhy. Fig. 1B

mp *w/pick and fingers*

Elec. Gtr. 2 tacet

flipped the beat, move___ the sheep like the shep - herd. It's a new___

F#m^{type2}

— day,   my   crew   stay   for - ev - er striv   -   ing.   Give   thanks__ 'cause we a -

live   and__   been through the gut - ter.   Now   we   see   the   ho - ri - zon.   It's

w/Rhy. Fig. 1B *(Acous. Gtr. 1)*

Em7

clear   to   me   now.__   Used to be con-fused, took a   lot   of years to see how.__   Now,   we mov-ing plan - ets.

F#m

Horns

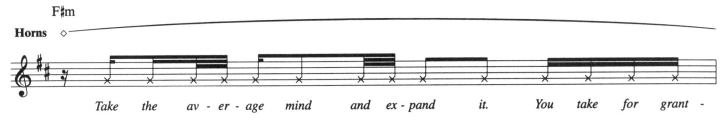

Take   the   av - er - age   mind   and   ex - pand   it.   You   take   for   grant -

w/Rhy. Figs. 1 *(Horns)*, **1A** *(Elec. Gtr. 2)*, **& 1B** *(Acous. Gtr. 1)*
2 times, simile

Em7

ed   like we're al - ways gon-na be dis - ad - van - taged. But soon come,   it   soon   come,__ it soon done.   Ya

start run, ya stum - ble,___ we catch one. *In the rhy-thm, San-ta-na lick the guits with pre-cis-ion. Not*

ac-ci-den-tal, in-ten-tion-al con-scious de-cis-ion. To Zi-on we're march-ing through with Af-ri-can May-ans.

Con - quer - ing Bab - y - lon with the heart of a li - on. Be -

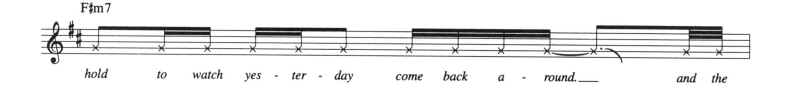

hold to watch yes - ter - day come back a - round.___ and the

Chorus:
w/Vocal Fig. 1 *(simile)*
w/Rhy. Figs. 1 *(Horns)* **& 1A** *(Elec. Gtr. 2) 2 times, simile*

walls of Jer - i - cho come a tumb-ling down.___ Se - lah   Ah, ah.___

Se - lah___

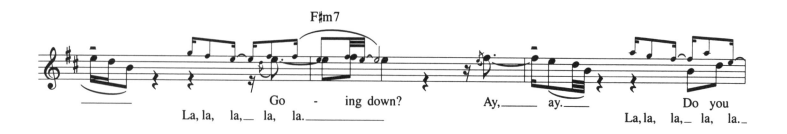

___   Go - ing down?   Ay,___ ay.___   Do you

La, la, la,___ la, la.___   La, la, la,___ la, la.

like the way,   Oh, yeah,___   that it's go - ing down?___

La, la, la.___

Do You Like the Way - 12 - 4
0413B

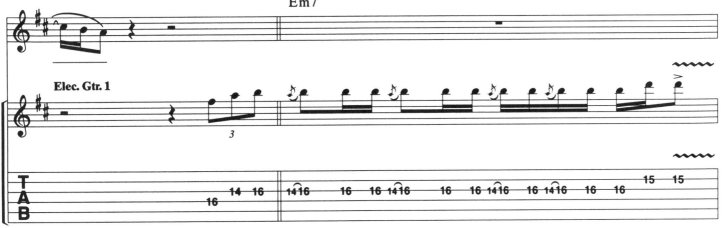

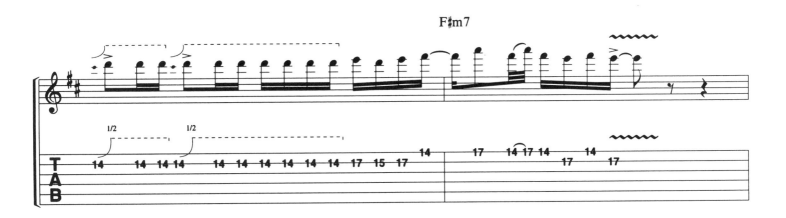

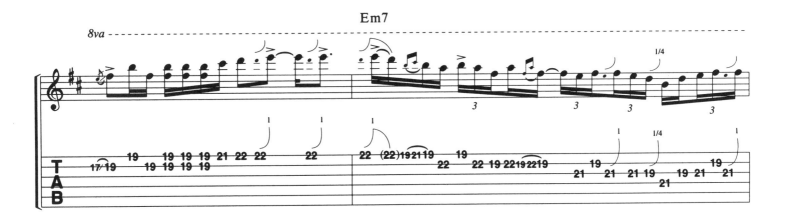

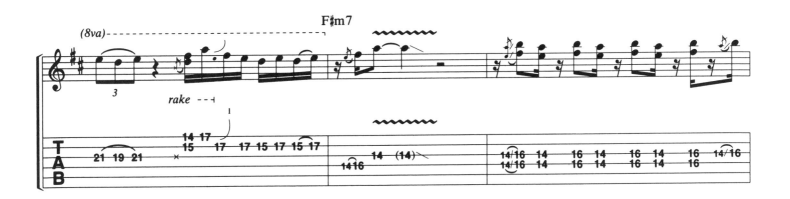

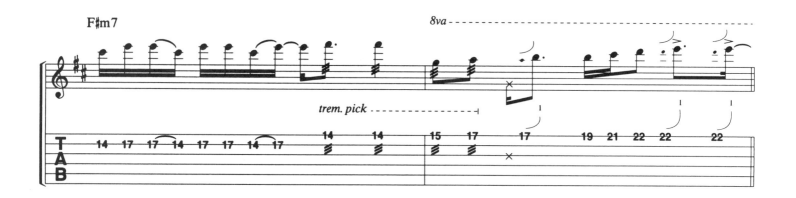

w/Rhy. Figs. 1 *(Horns)* **& 1A** *(Elec. Gtr. 2) 2 times, simile*

Do you like_ the way? Ah._____ Do you like_ the

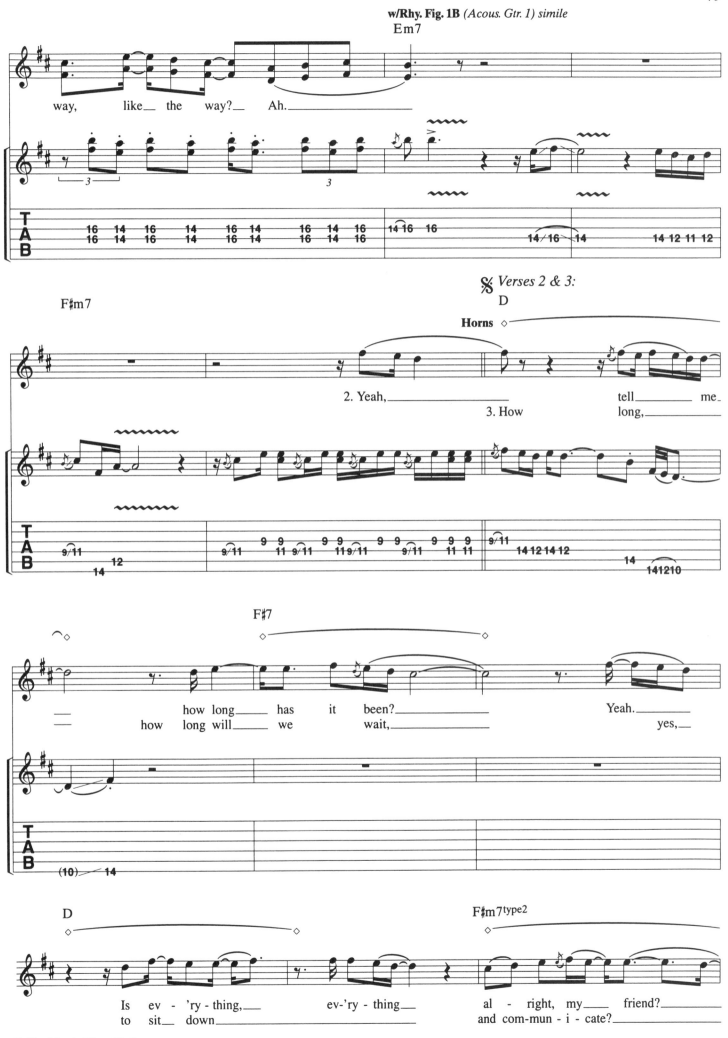

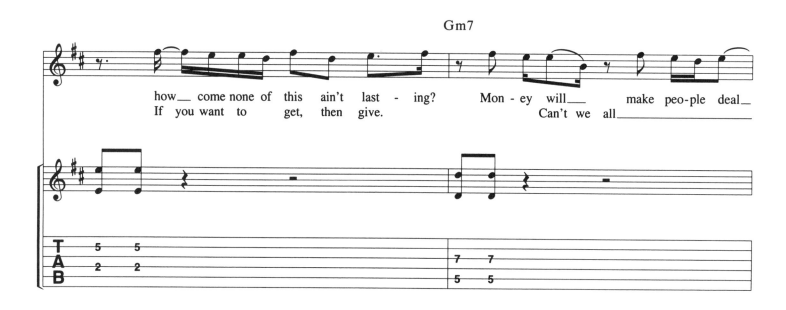

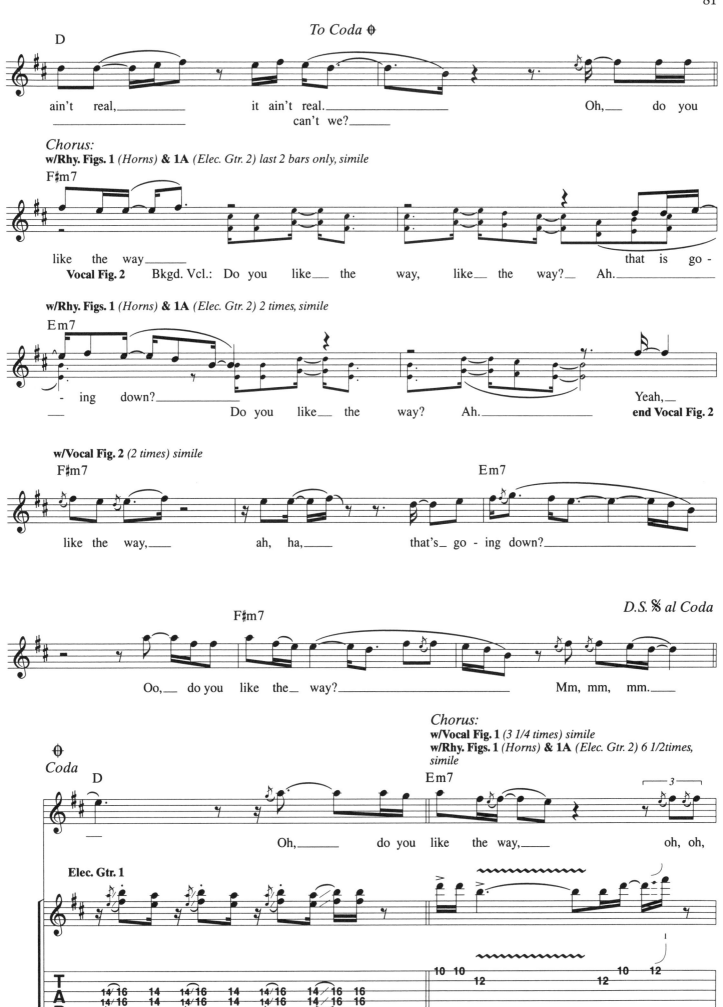

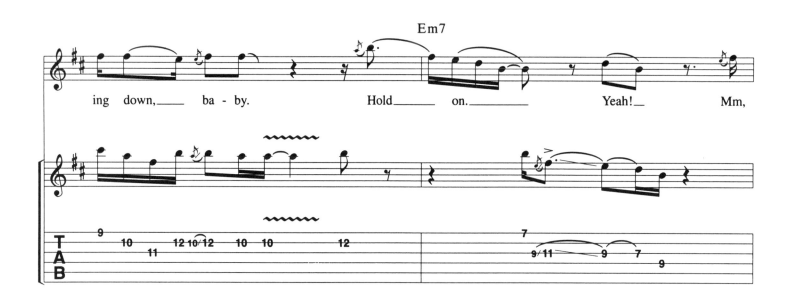

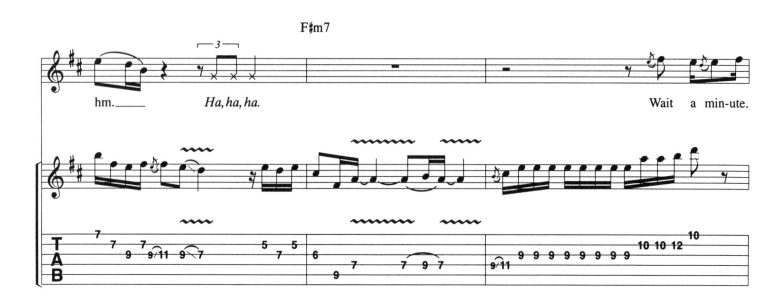

Lead Vocal tacet

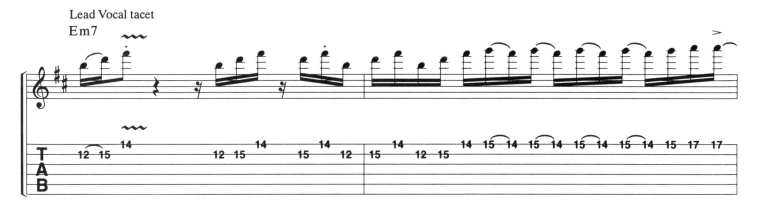

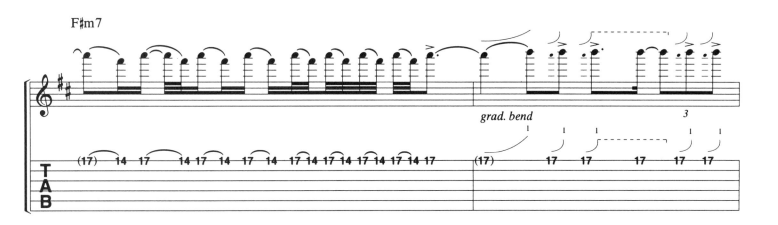

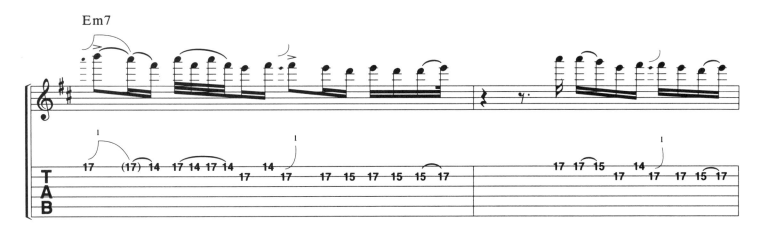

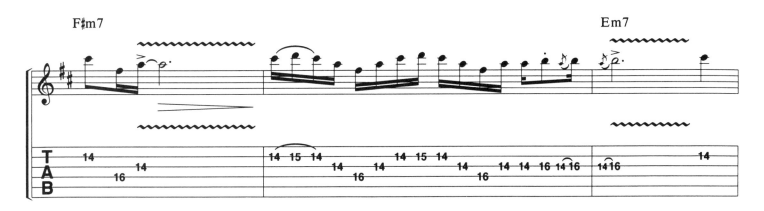

Do You Like the Way - 12 - 11
0413B

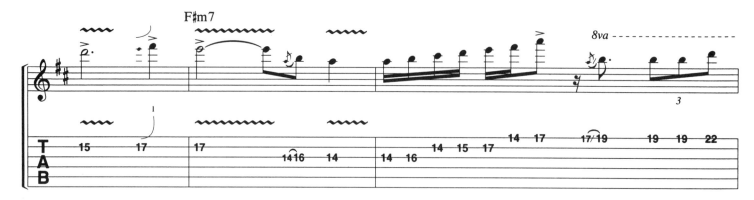

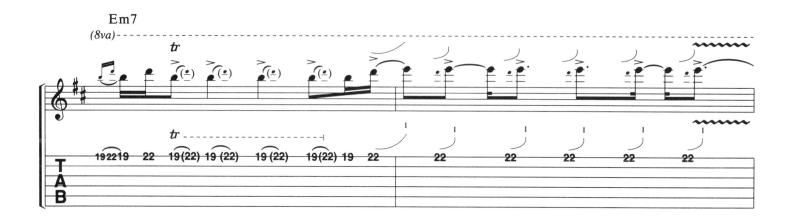

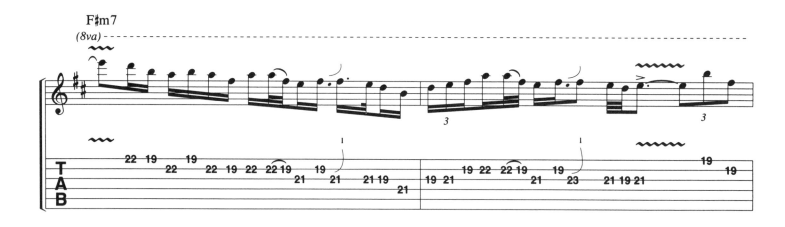

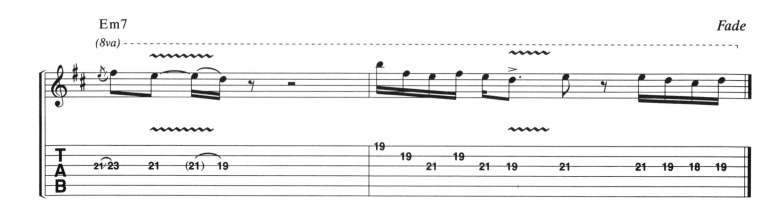

MARIA MARIA

Words and Music by
**WYCLEF JEAN, JERRY DUPLESSIS,
CARLOS SANTANA, KARL PERAZZO and RAUL REKOW**

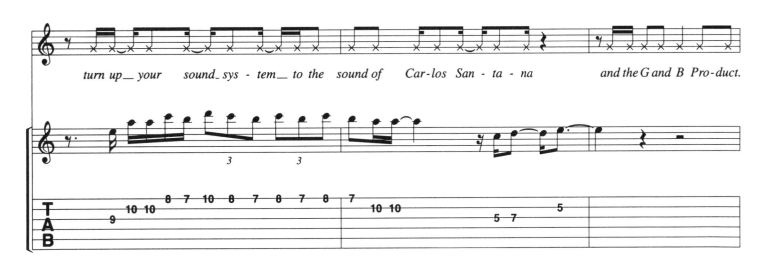

Maria Maria - 16 - 1
0413B

Stop the loot-

-ing, stop the shoot-ing, pick-pock-ing on__ the cor-ner. See, as the rich__

Verse 1:
Am

G

Keybd.
Rhy. Fig. 3A

Rhy. Fig. 3

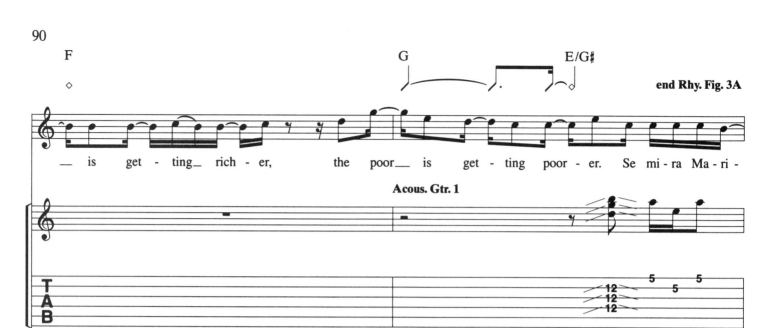

She's liv-ing the life__ just like__ a mov-ie star._____ Oh,_____ Ma - ri - a, Ma - ri -

a,_____ she fell in love in east__L. A.,_____

I said it to the sounds__ of a__ gui - tar,__ yeah,__ yeah,_____ played by__ Car - los__ San - ta -

w//Rhy. Fig. 1 *(Bass) 2 times, simile*

Am

- na.

Elec. Gtr. 1

Verse 2:

Am7　　　　　　　　　　　　　　G

Keybd.

I said a la fa-vel - la　los co-lo - res.　The streets are get - ting hot - ter. There is no wa-

Bass

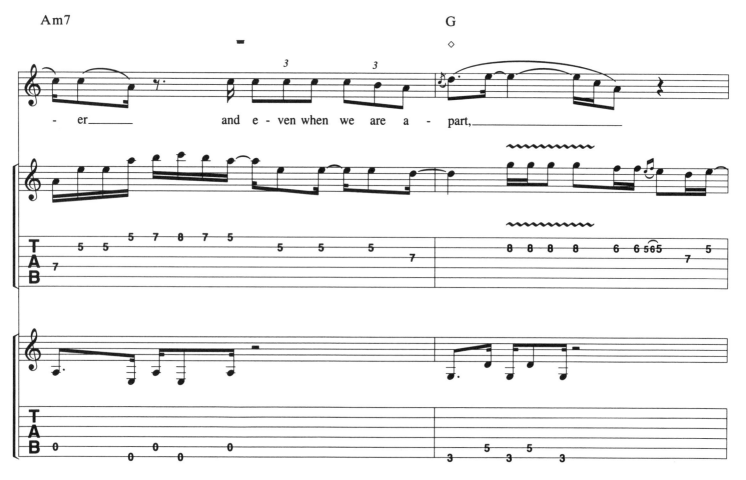

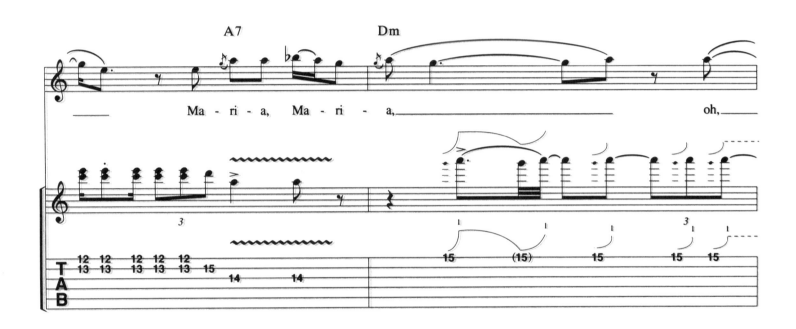

Slow fade

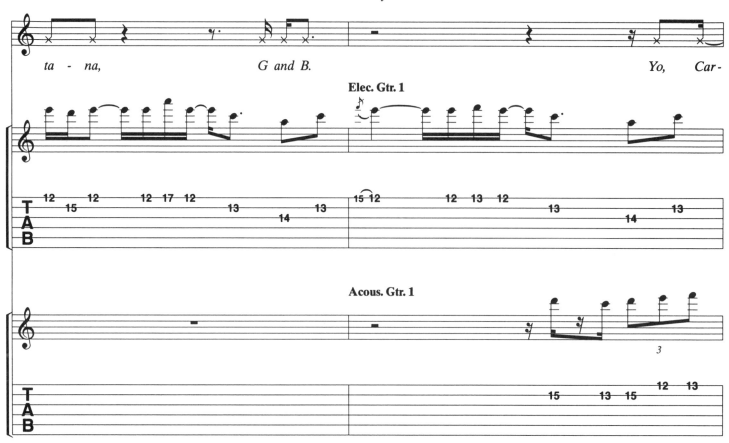

Fade

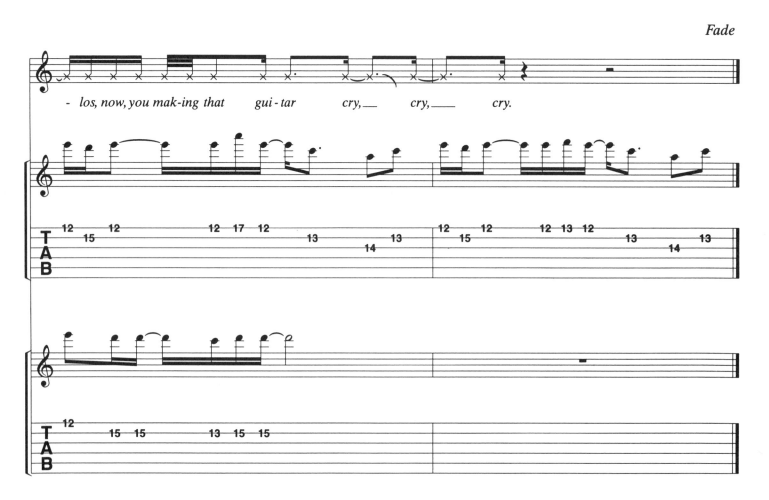

MIGRA

Words and Music by
RACHID TAHA, CARLOS SANTANA and TONY LINDSAY

Moderately ♩ = 108

Intro:

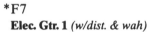

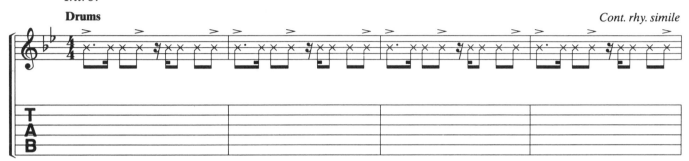

*Entire song based in the tonality of F Mixolydian/F min. pentatonic.

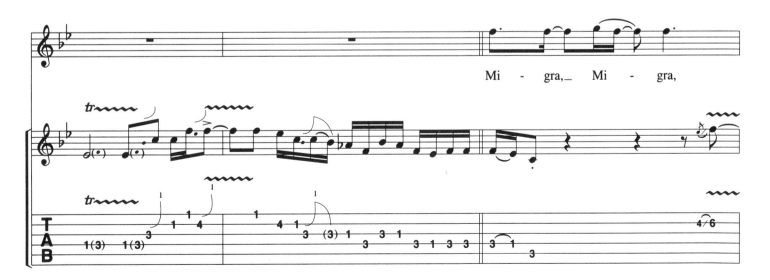

Mi - gra,_ Mi - gra,

Migra - 14 - 1
0413B

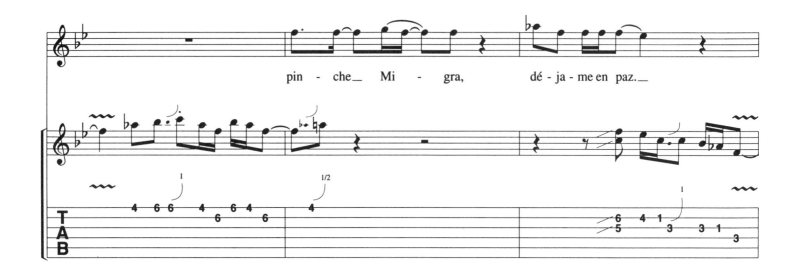

pin - che_ Mi - gra,   dé - ja - me en paz._

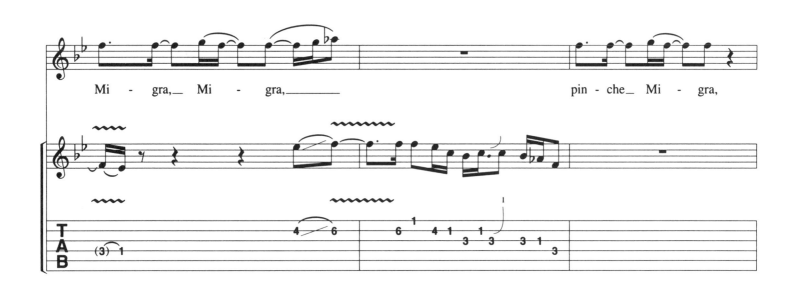

Mi - gra,_ Mi - gra,_____   pin - che_ Mi - gra,

de - ja - me en paz._   Ma - li - cia en tus o - jos___   des -

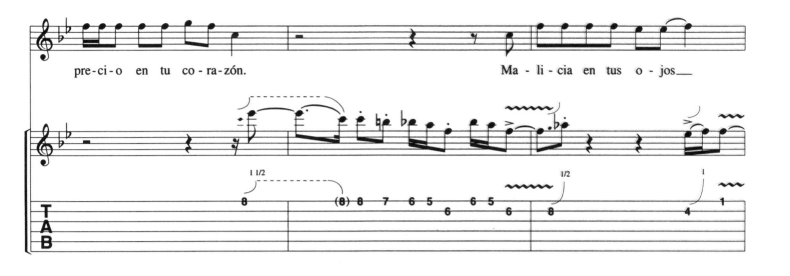

pre-ci-o en tu co-ra-zón.

Ma - li - cia en tus o - jos___

des - pre-ci-o en tu co-ra-zón.

Es

ho - ra de re - co - no - cer

que to-dos so-mos u - na voz.

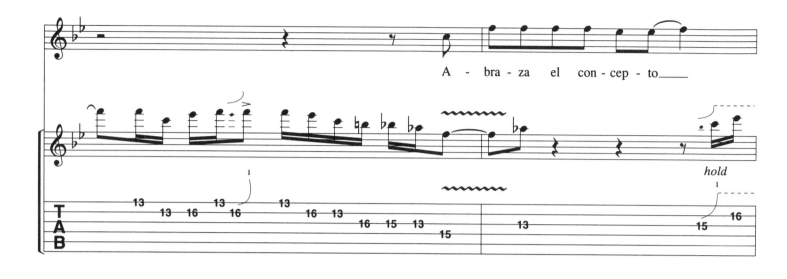

A - bra - za el con - cep - to____

hold

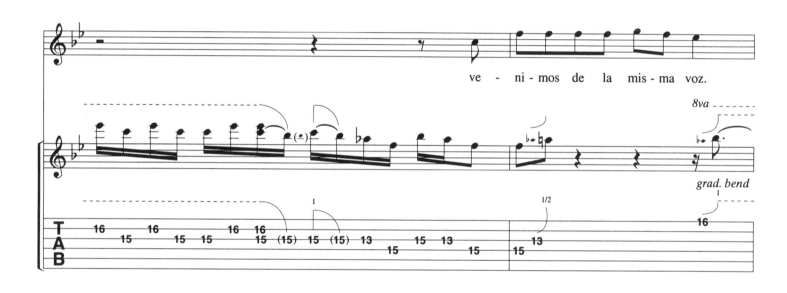

ve - ni - mos de la mis - ma voz.

8va

grad. bend

Chorus:

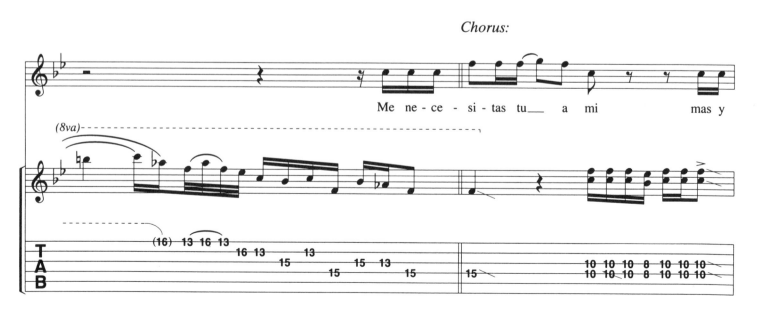

Me ne - ce - si - tas tu____ a mi mas y

mas que yo_ a ti. Me ne-ce - si - tas tu_ a mi mas y mas que yo_ a ti. Me ne-ce-

si - tas tu_ a mi mas y mas que yo_ a ti. Me ne-ce - si - tas tu_ a mi mas y

Interlude:

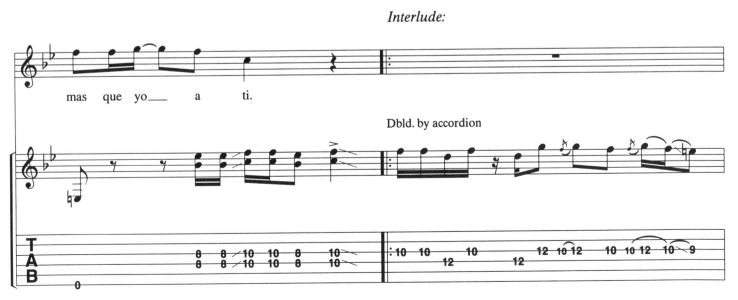

mas que yo___ a ti.

Dbld. by accordion

Play 4 times

Peo - ple,_ peo - ple,   let's

start to - geth - er. Let's do it right now._   Peo - ple, peo - ple,_____

let's love one_ an - oth - er,   I know we know how._

Dbld. by trumpet

Trumpet *(arr. for gtr.)*

mf

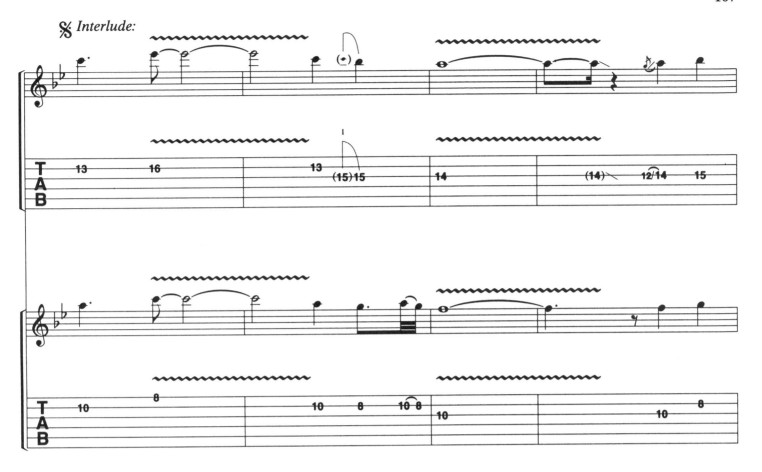

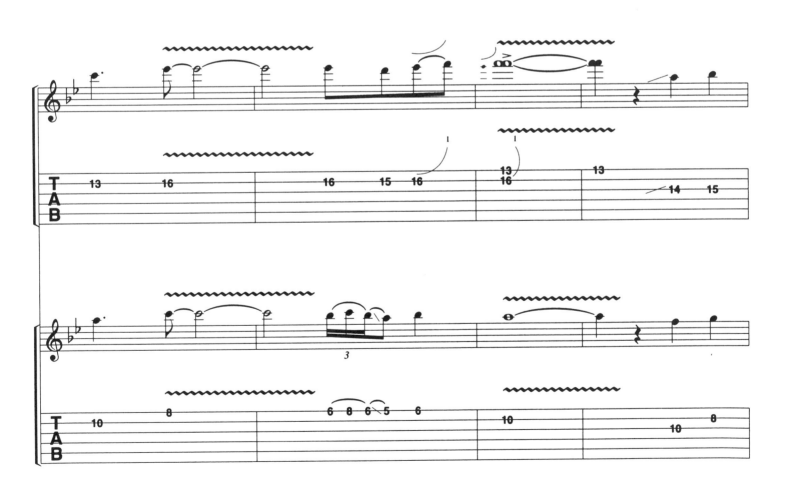

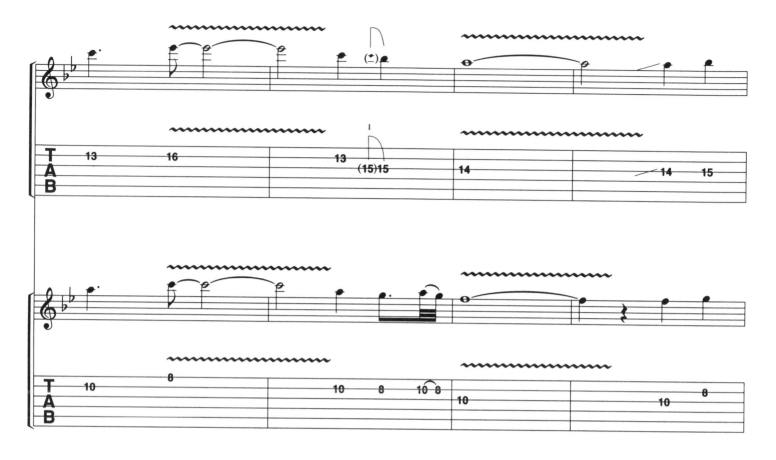

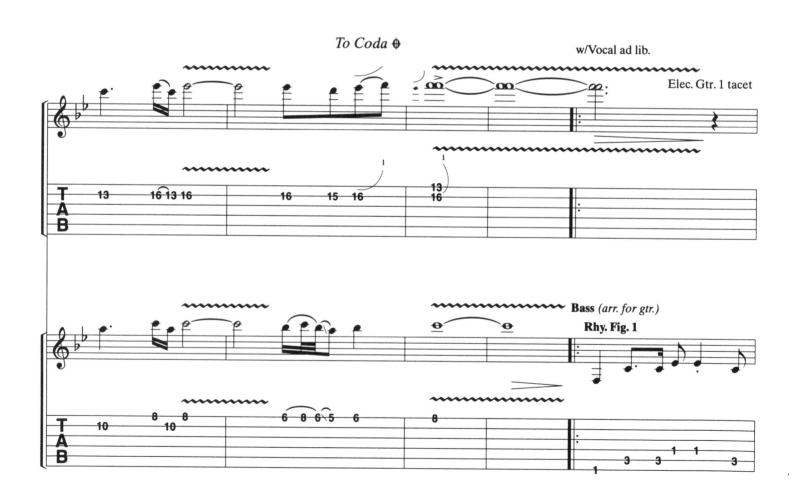

Guitar Solo:
w/Rhy. Fig. 1 *(Bass) 4 times, simile*

Elec. Gtr. 1

f *w/wah*

w/bar

w/bar

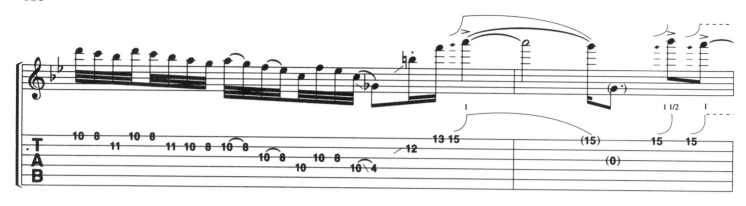

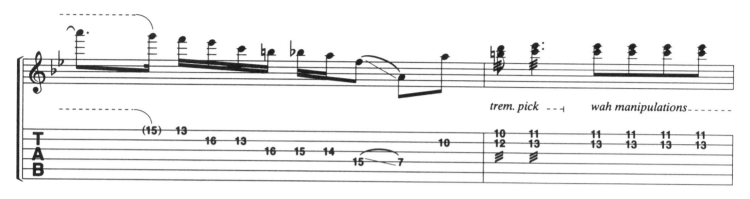

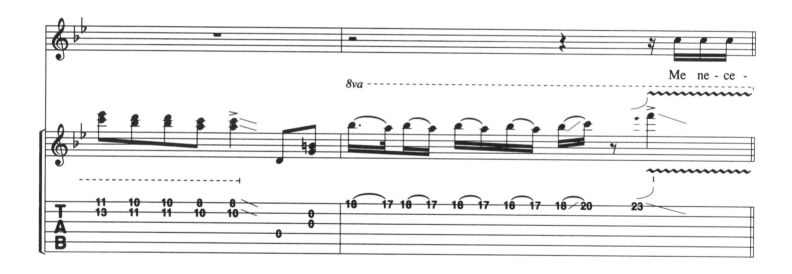

Chorus:

si - tas tu___ a mi mas y mas que yo___ a ti. Me ne - ce -

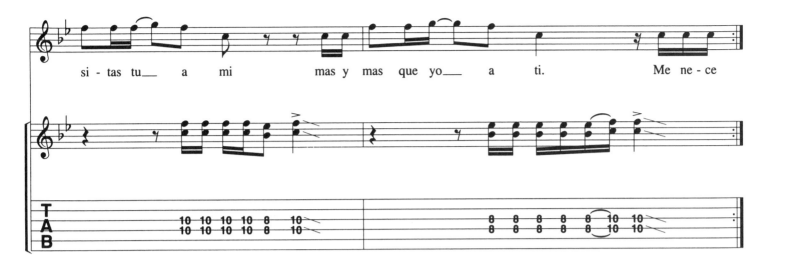

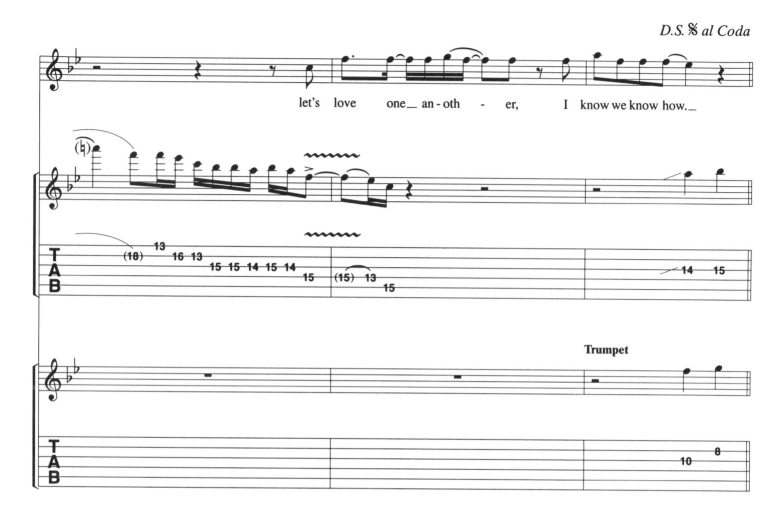

let's love one_ an - oth - er, I know we know how._

Coda

Interlude:
F9

w/wah

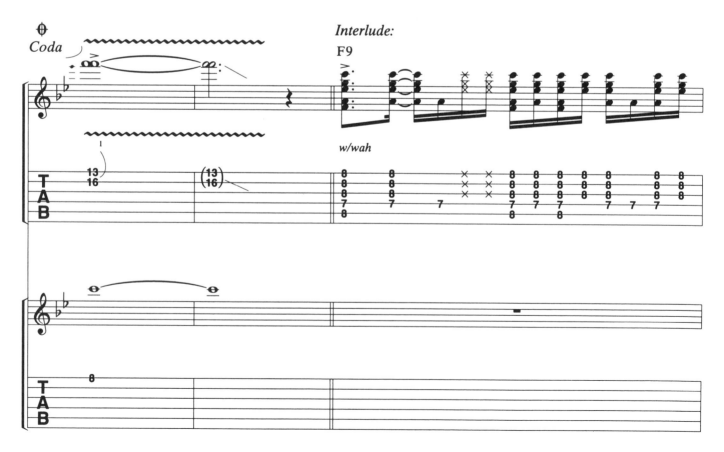

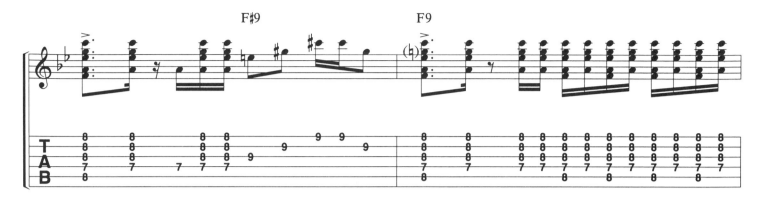

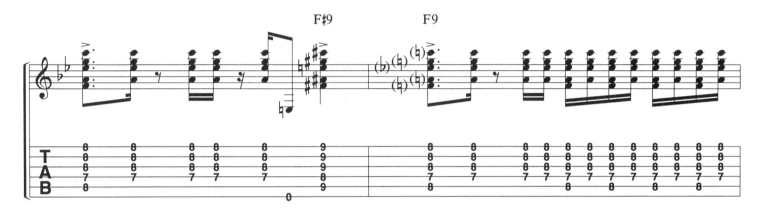

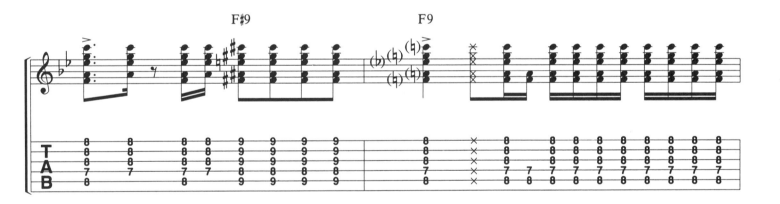

Outro:

CORAZON ESPINADO

Words and Music by
FHER OLVERA

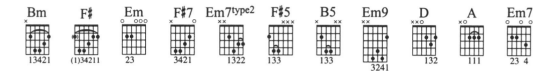

Moderately fast ♩ = 120
Intro:

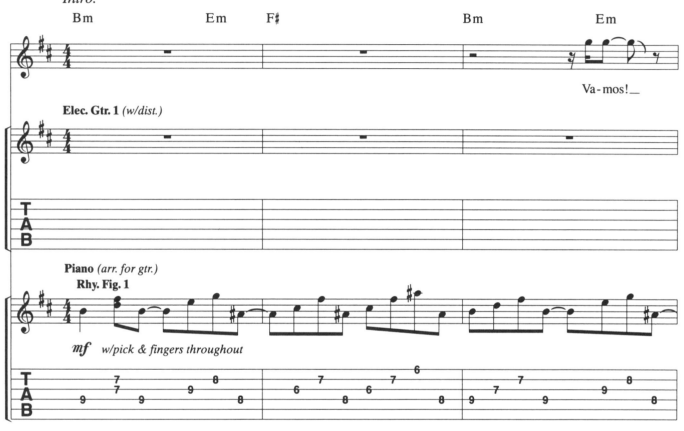

Va-mos!

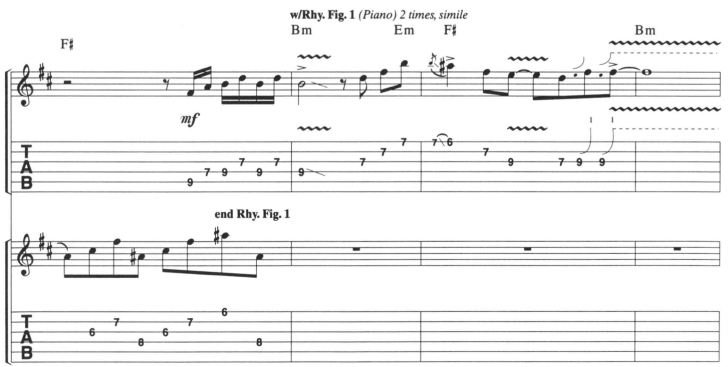

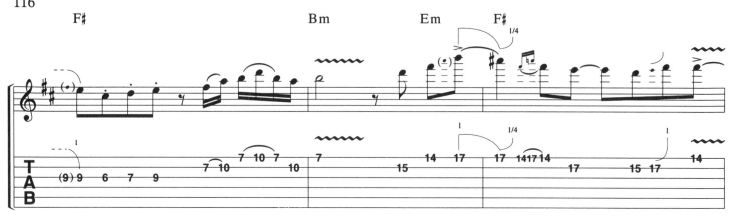

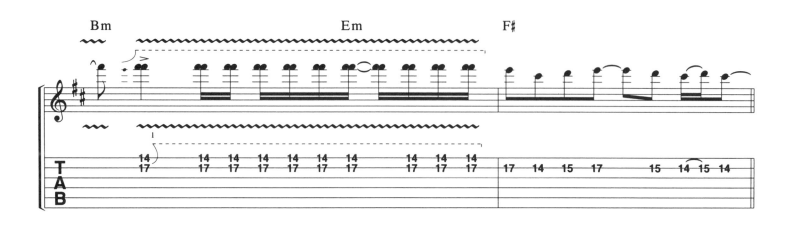

Verse 1:

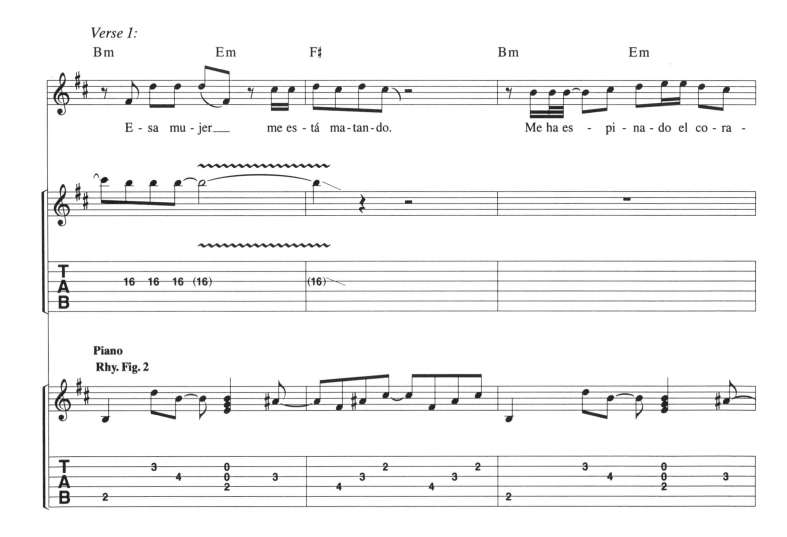

E - sa mu - jer___ me es - tá ma - tan - do. Me ha es - pi - na - do el co - ra -

- me mi a - mor,___ por fa - vor. Y qué do - lor nos que - dó.

Chorus:

w/Rhy. Figs. 3 *(Piano)* & 3A
(Elec. Gtr. 2) 3 times, simile

Ah, ah, hay, co - ra - zón es - pi - na - do. Co - mo due - le, me due-

le el a - mor. Ah, ah, hay, co - mo me due - le el a - mor.

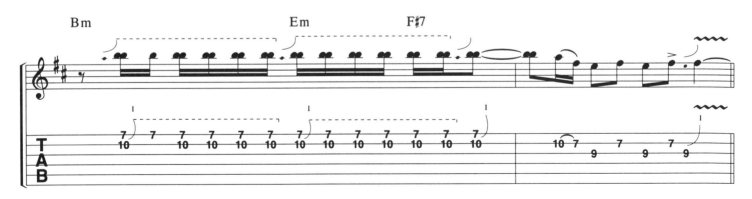

Verse 2:
w/Rhy. **Fig. 2** *(Piano) 2 times, simile*

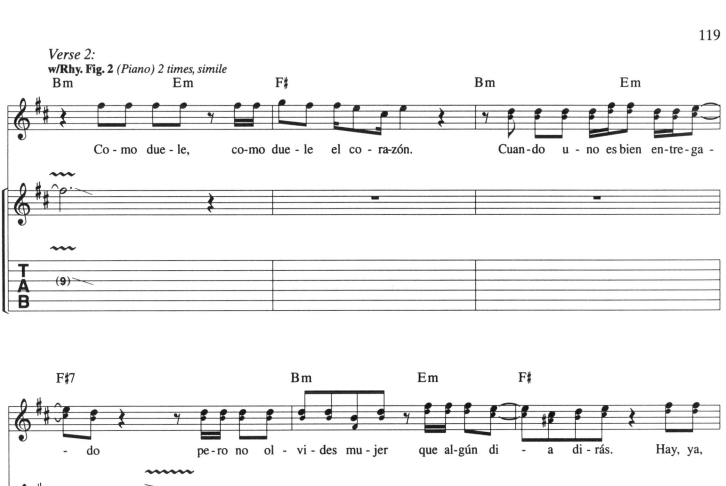

Co - mo due - le, co-mo due - le el co - ra-zón. Cuan-do u - no es bien en-tre-ga-

-do pe-ro no ol - vi-des mu-jer que al-gún di - a di-rás. Hay, ya,

Chorus:
w/Rhy. **Figs. 3** *(Piano)* & **3A**
(Elec. Gtr. 2) 7 times, simile

yay co-mo me due - le el a-mor. Ah, ah, hay,

co - ra-zón es - pi-na - do. Co-mo due - le, me due - le el a-mor. Ah, ah, hay,

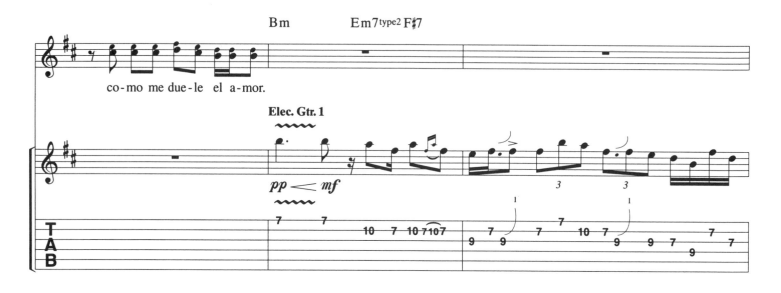

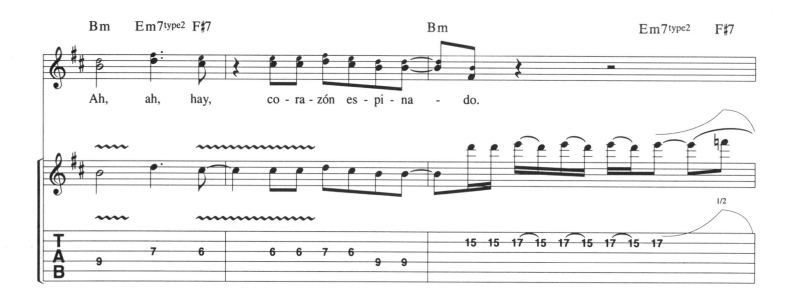

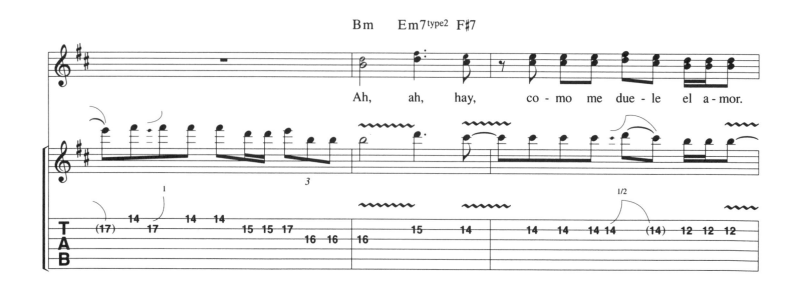

Guitar Solo:

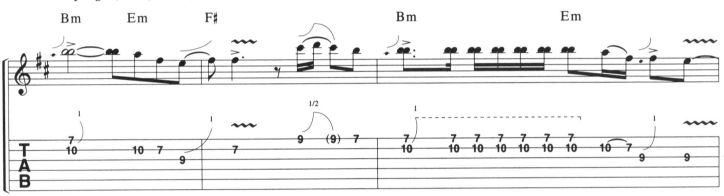

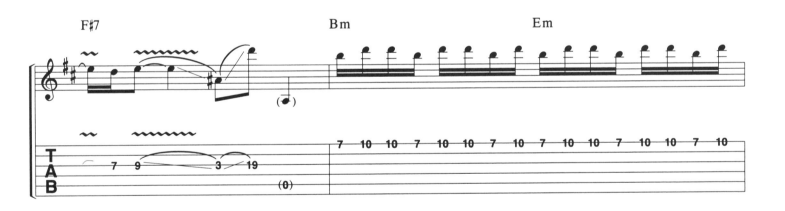

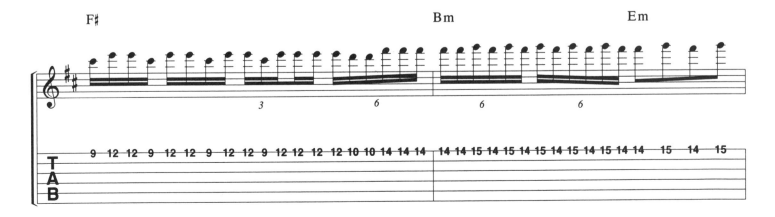

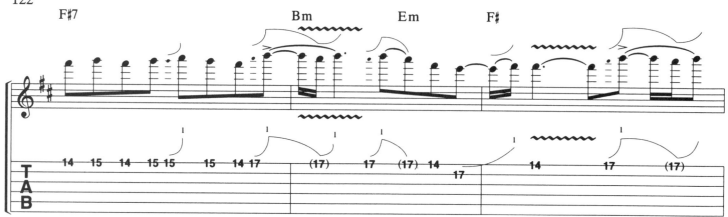

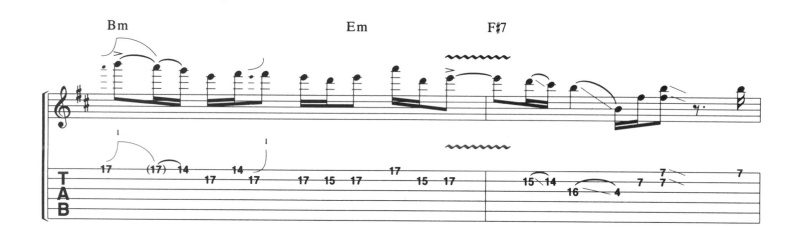

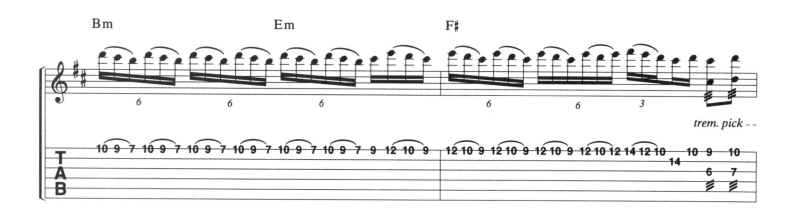

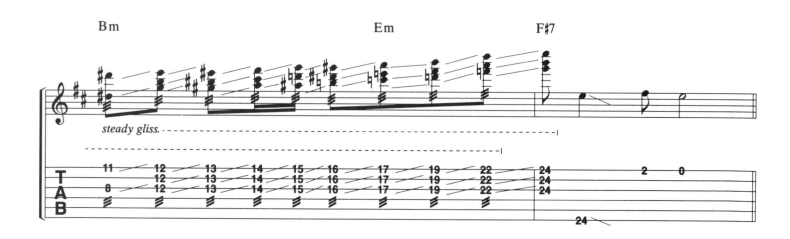

124

Corazon Espinado - 15 - 10
0413B

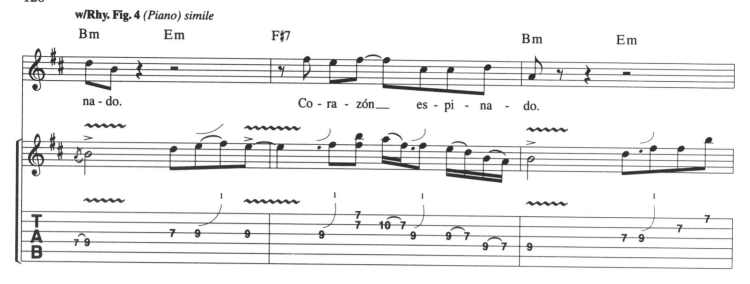

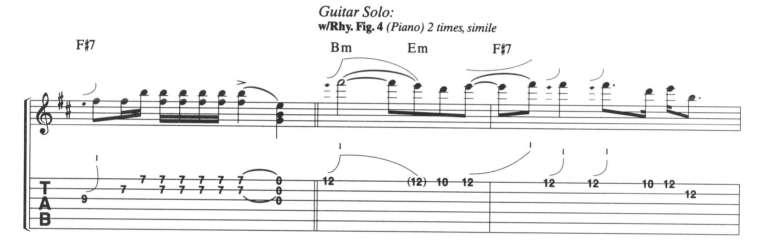

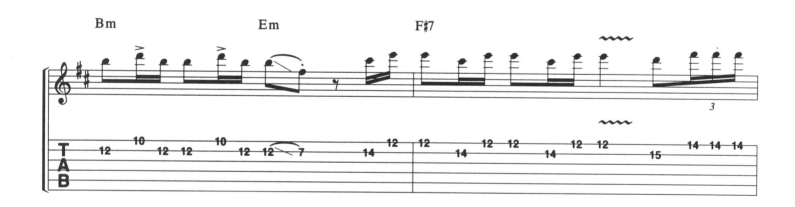

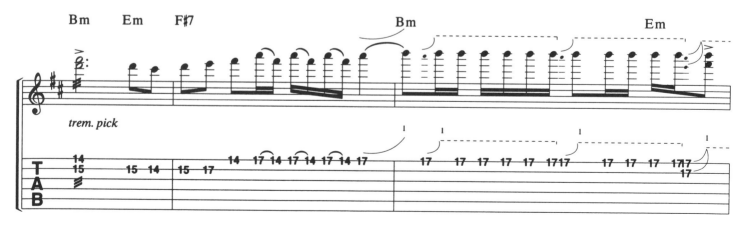

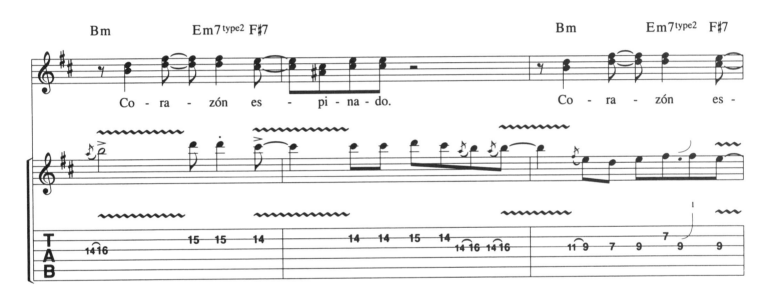

Chorus:
w/Rhy. Fig. 3 (Piano) *4 times, simile*

Co - ra - zón es - pi - na - do.

Co - ra - zón es - pi - na - do.

Co - ra - zón es -

- pi - na - do.

Co - ra - zón es - pi - na - do.

Corazon Espinado - 15 - 13
0413B

Outro:
w/Rhy. Fig. 3 *(Piano) 8 times, simile ad lib.*

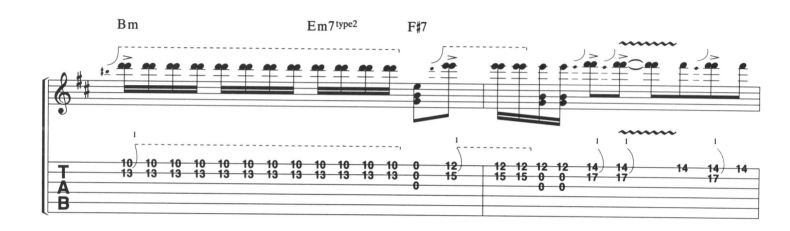

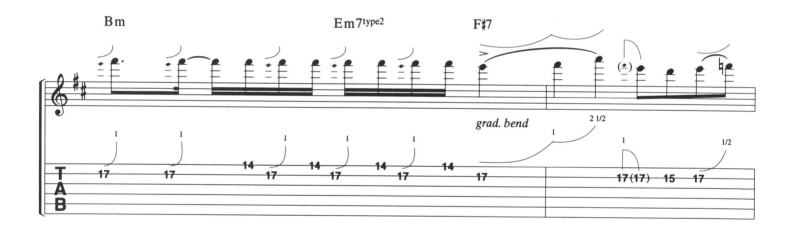

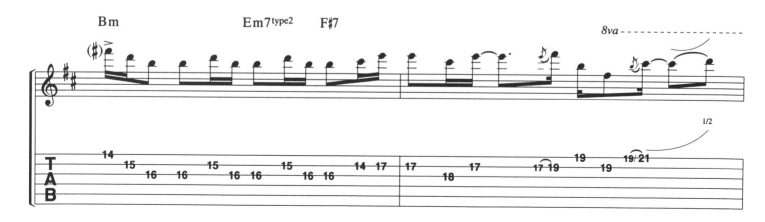

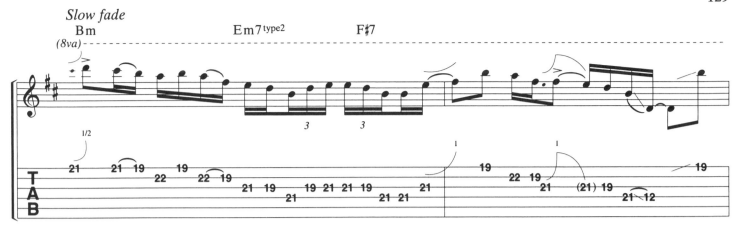

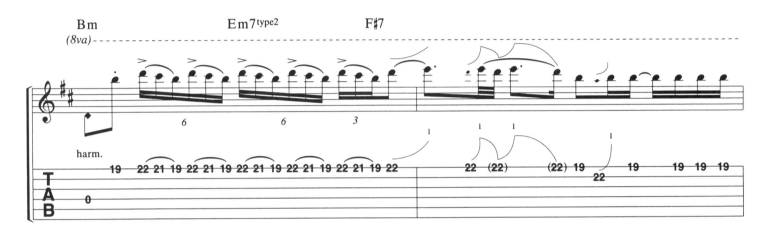

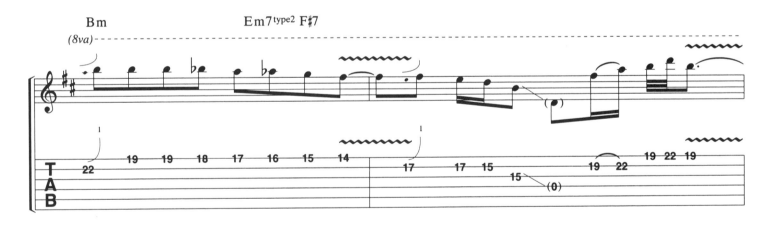

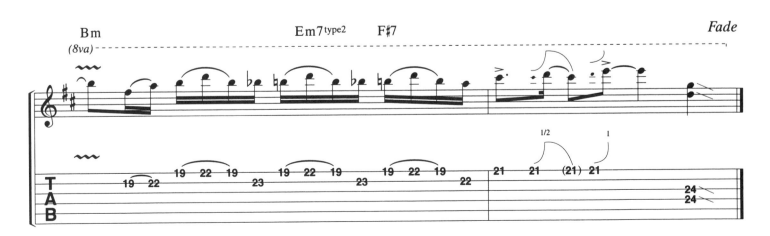

Corazon Espinado - 15 - 15
0413B

WISHING IT WAS

Words and Music by
EAGLE-EYE CHERRY, MICHAEL SIMPSON,
JON KING and MARK NISHITA

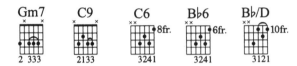

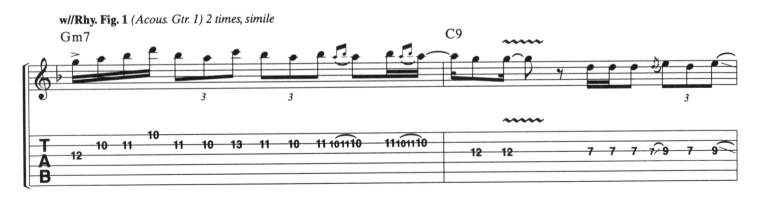

Wishing It Was - 11 - 1
0413B

Verses 1 & 2:
w/Rhy. Fig. 1 *(Acous. Gtr. 1) 4 times, simile*
w/Lead Fig. 1 *(Elec. Gtr. 2) 2 times, simile (Verse 2 only)*

1. Beau - ty and grace is what touch - es me most. Good times can put me in fear. I
(2.) feel - ing won't last, 'cause I can - not sur - vive. I tell you I've been here be - fore. I'm
di - di.

Elec. Gtr. 1 *(Verse 2 only)*

al - ways feel safe when things_ are bad.__ So I can - not let you come near. It
mov - ing so fast, it's a mat - ter of time. One of us walks out that door. It

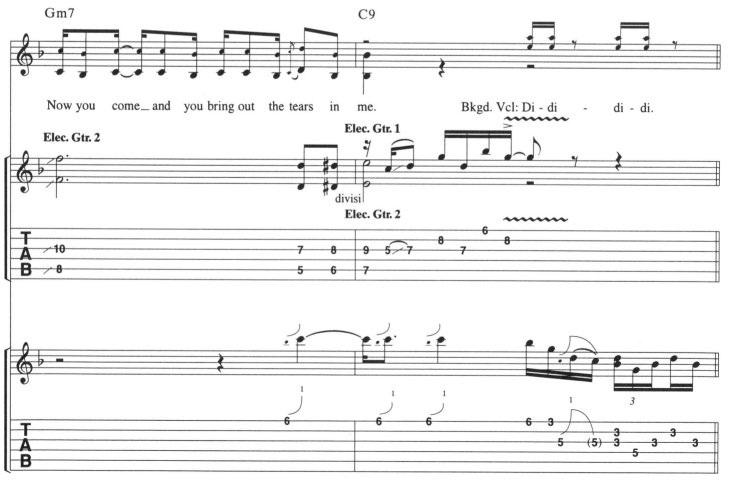

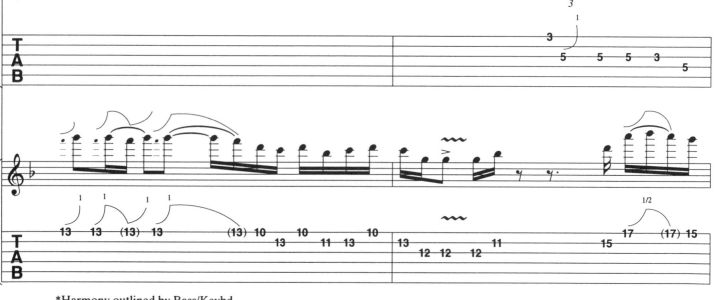

*Harmony outlined by Bass/Keybd.

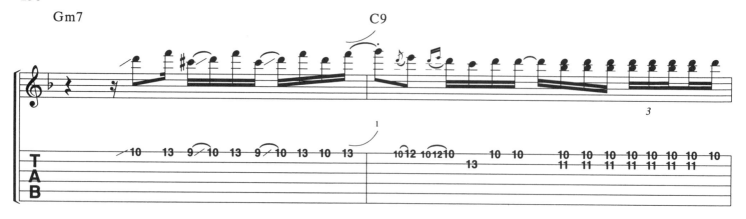

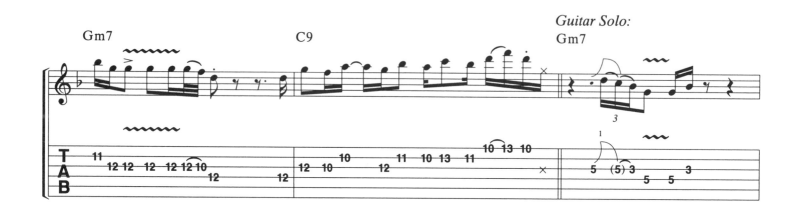

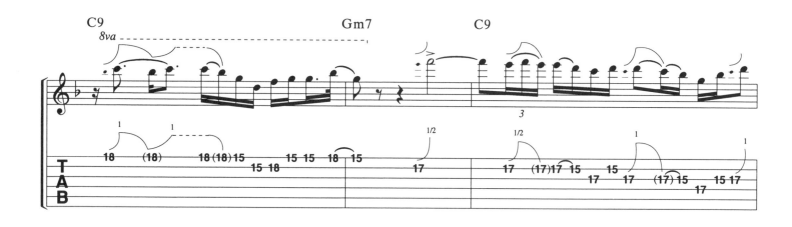

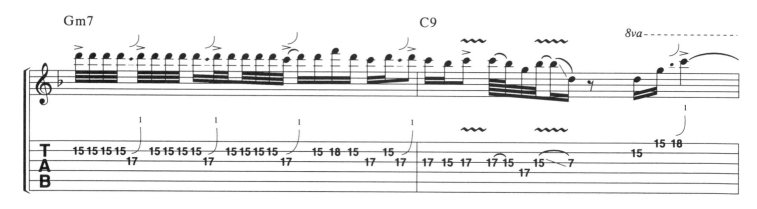

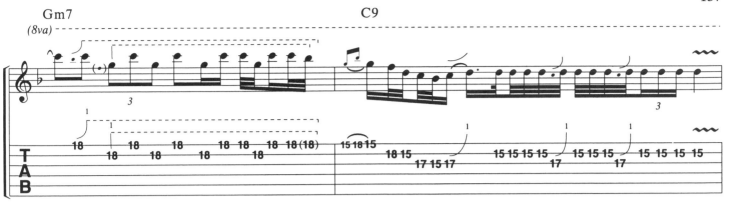

w/Lead Fig. 1 *(Elec. Gtr. 2) 2 times, simile*

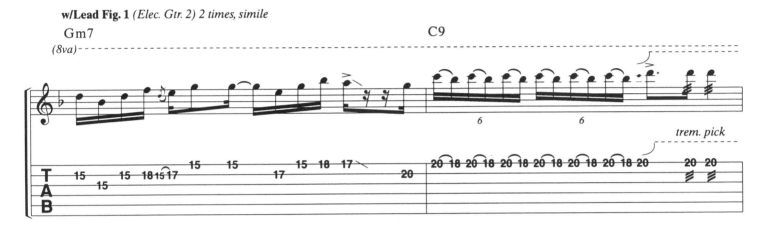

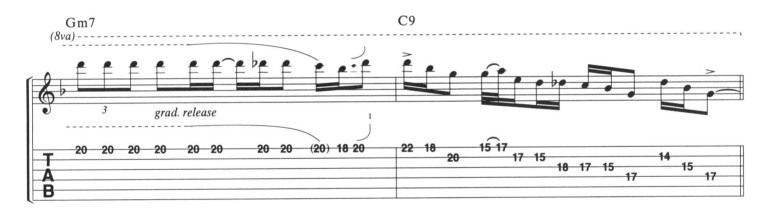

Verse 3:
w/Rhy. Fig. 1 *(Acous. Gtr. 1) 2 times, simile*

Give this some thought, I'm sure— you will know this is the way it must— be. E-

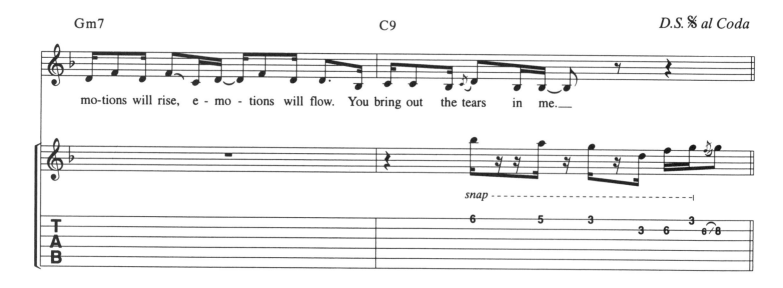

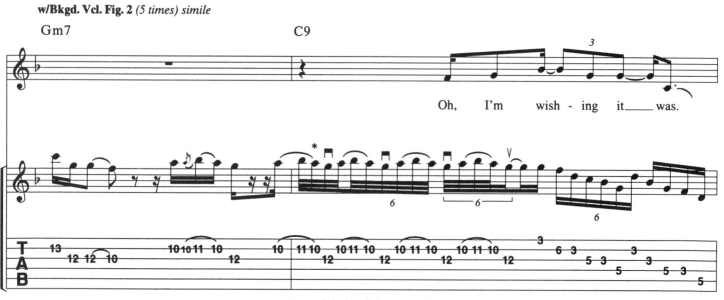

*⊓ = right hand down-stroke.
V = up-stroke.

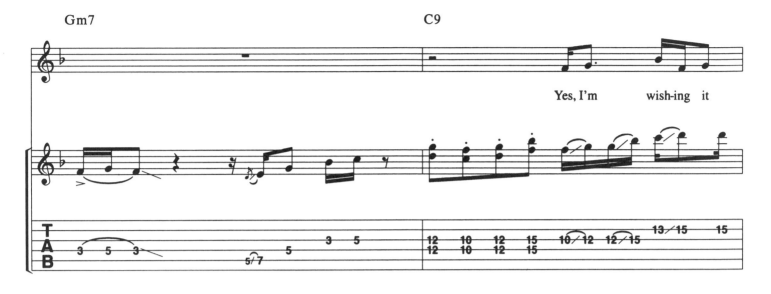

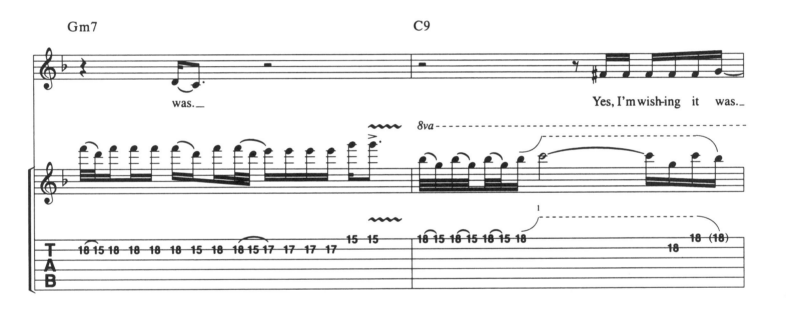

*Composite arrangement of Gtr. & Keybd.

EL FAROL

**Words and Music by
CARLOS SANTANA and K. C. PORTER**

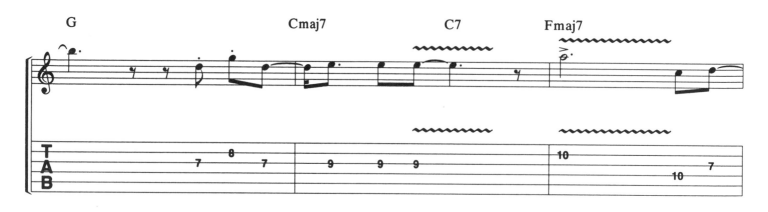

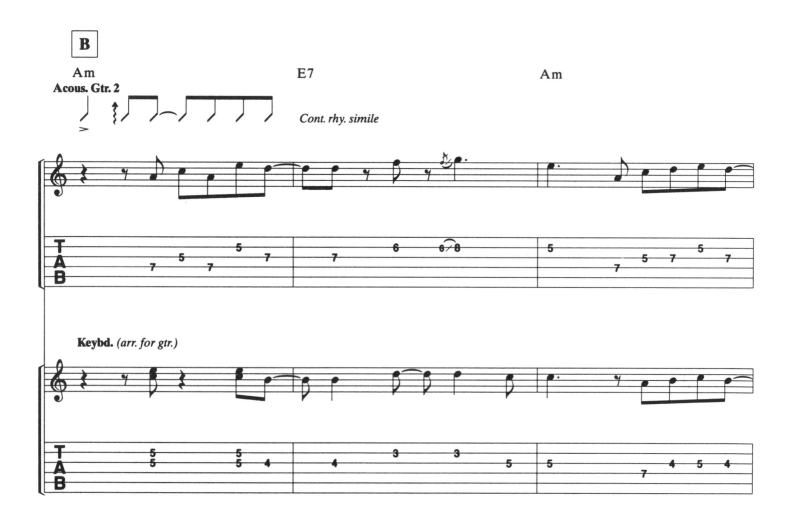

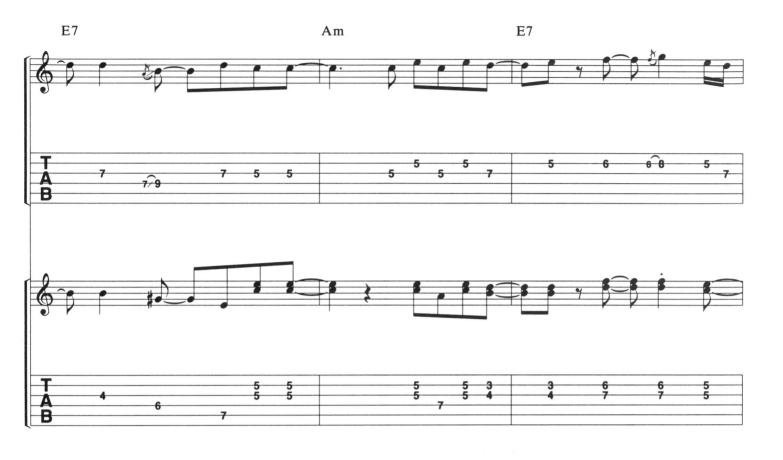

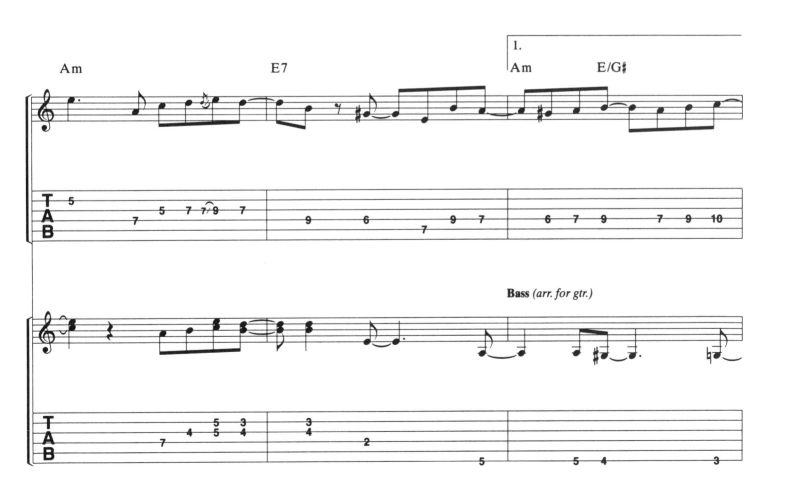

El Farol - 8 - 3
0413B

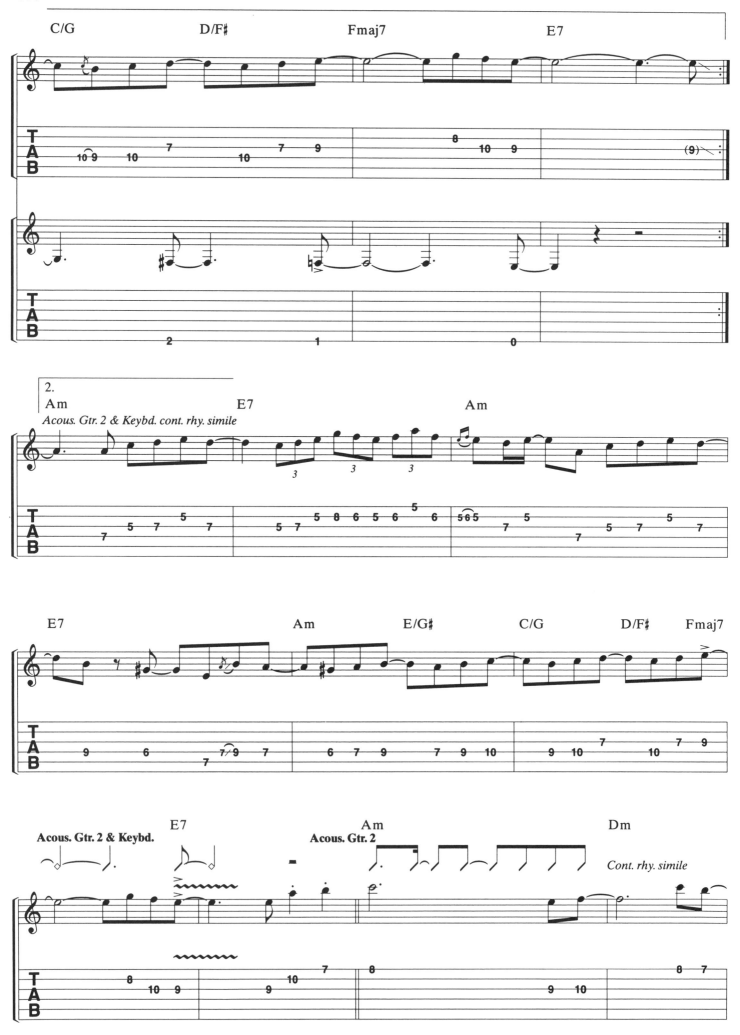

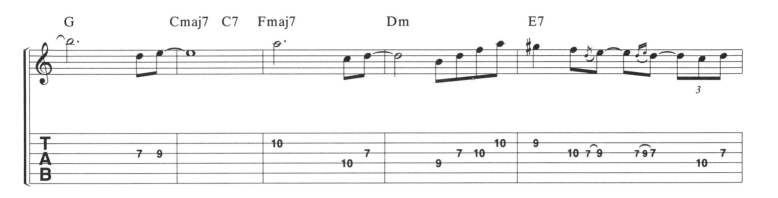

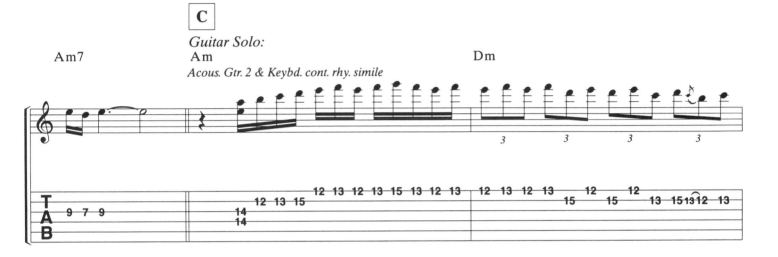

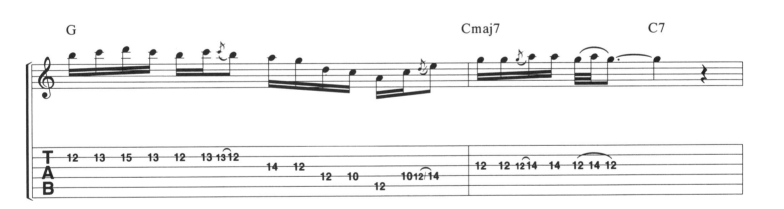

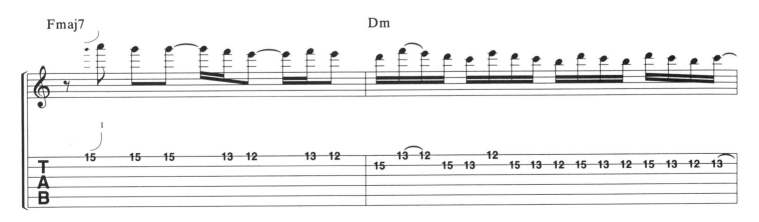

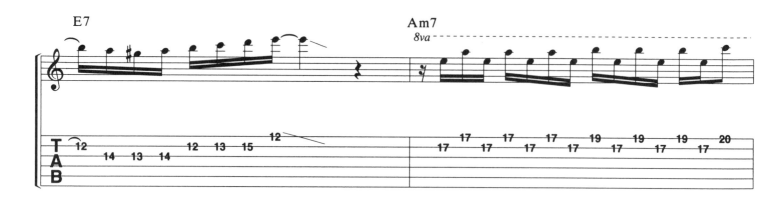

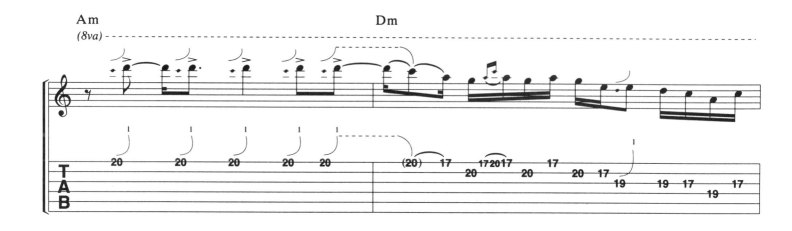

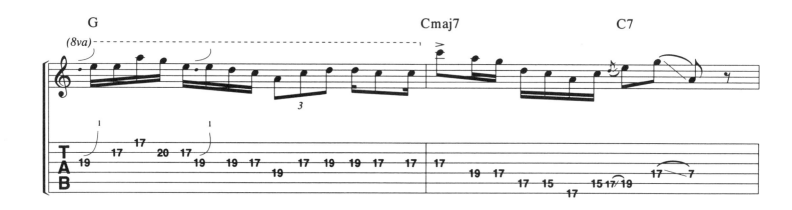

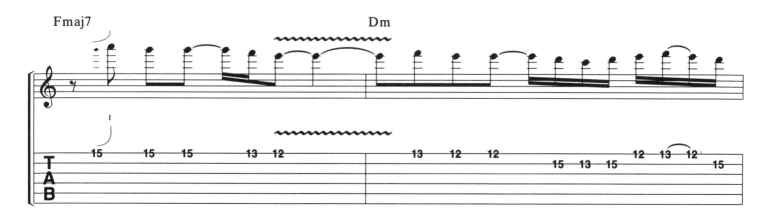

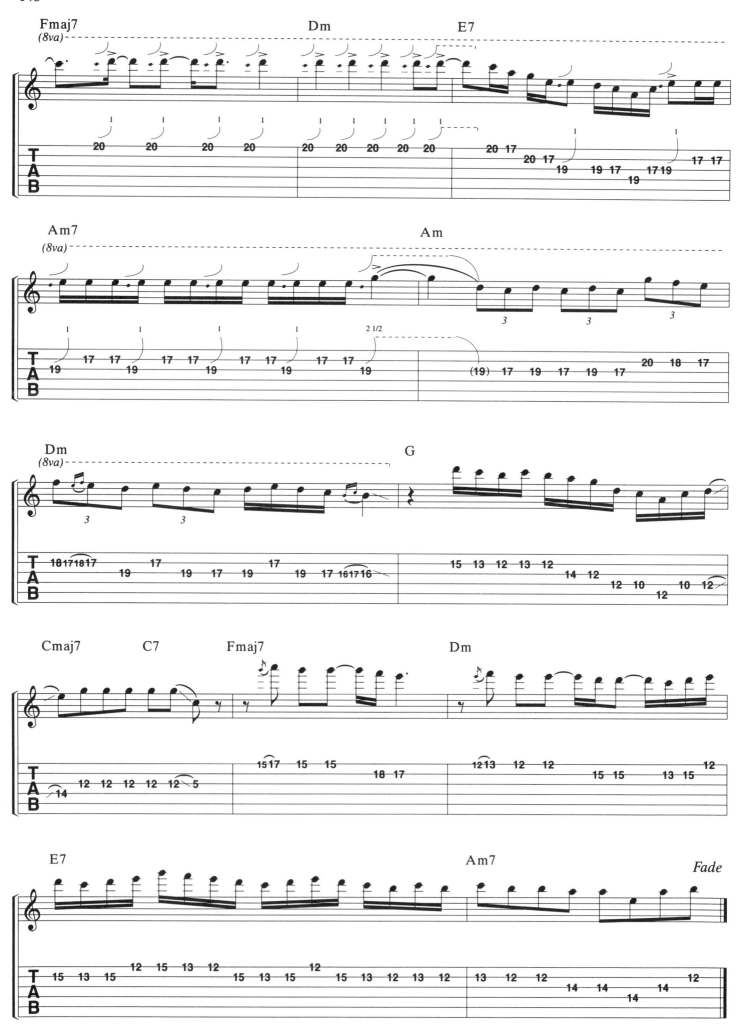

PRIMAVERA

Words and Music by
K. C. PORTER and J. B. ECKL

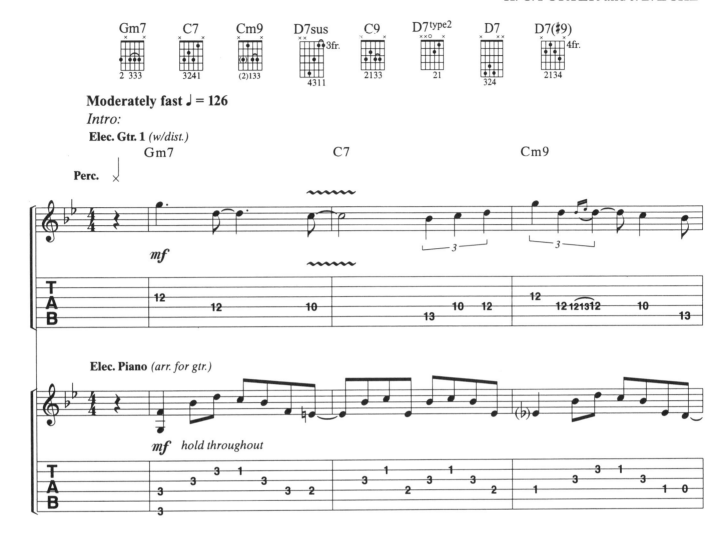

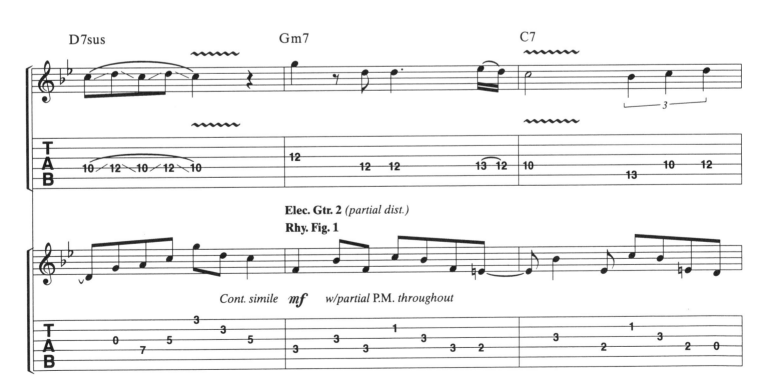

Primavera - 18 - 1
0413B

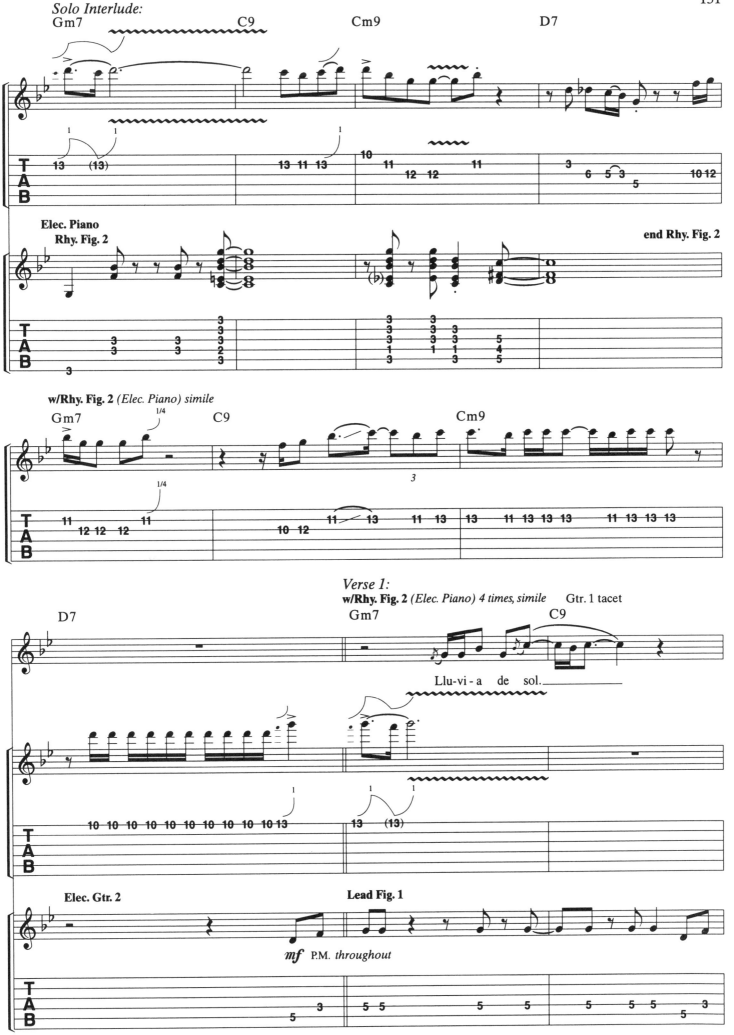

Chorus:
w/Rhy. Fig. 2 *(Elec. Piano) 4 times, simile*

Verse 2:
w/Rhy. Fig. 2 *(Elec. Piano) 2 times, simile*
w/Lead Fig. 1 *(Elec. Gtr. 2) 2 times, simile*

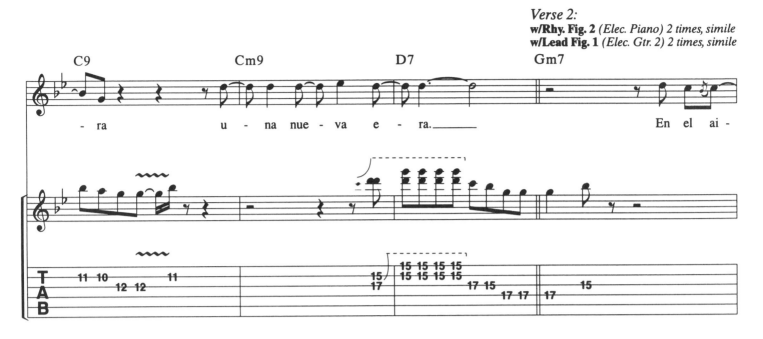

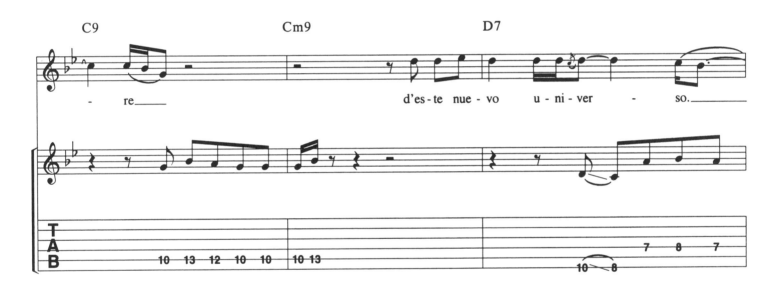

w/Bkgd. Vocal Fig. 1

% Pre-chorus:
w/Rhy. Fig. 2 *(Elec. Piano) 2 times, simile*
w/Lead Fig. 1 *(Elec. Gtr. 1) 2 times, simile*

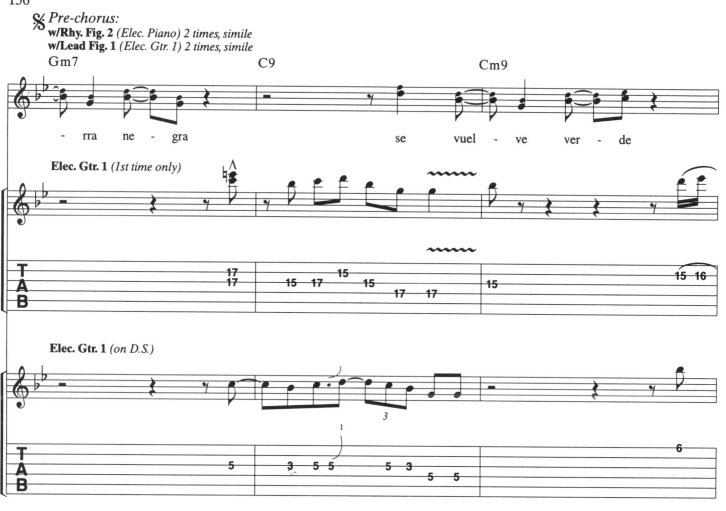

-rra ne - gra   se vuel - ve ver - de

Elec. Gtr. 1 *(1st time only)*

Elec. Gtr. 1 *(on D.S.)*

y   las___ mon - ta - ñas y el___ de - sier - to un___

in unison

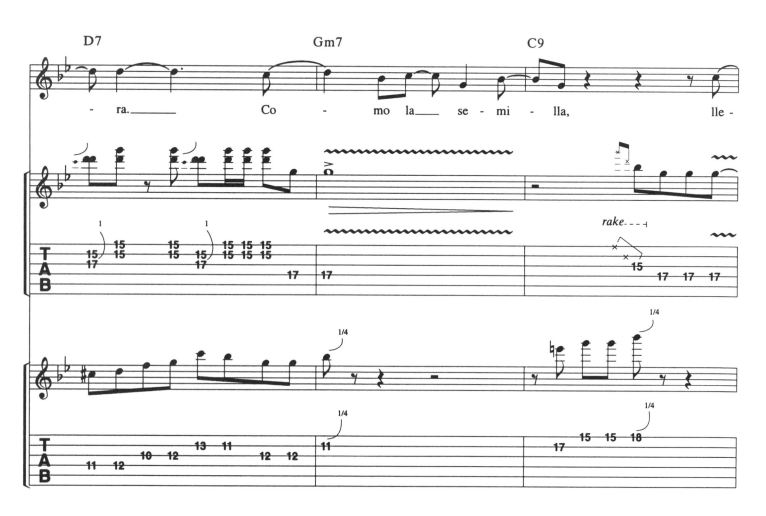

Guitar Solo:
w/Rhy. Fig. 2 *(Elec. Piano) 6 times, simile*
w/Lead Fig. 2 *(Elec. Gtr. 2) 6 times, simile*

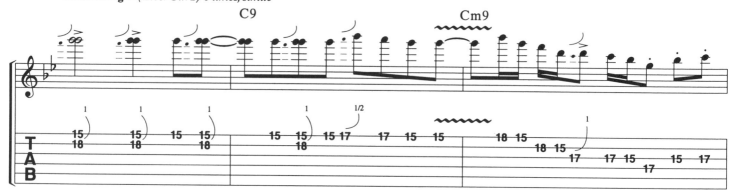

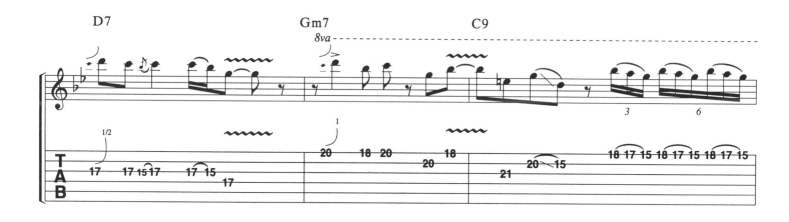

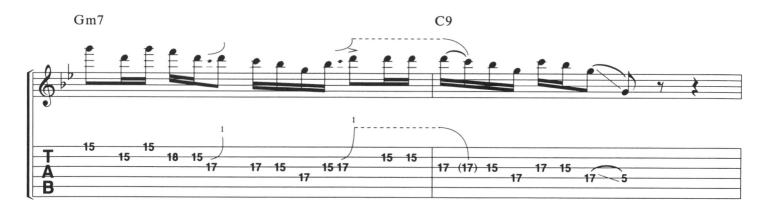

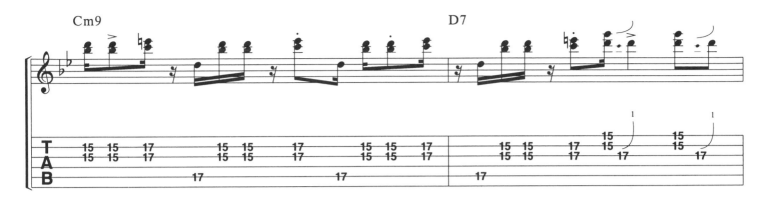

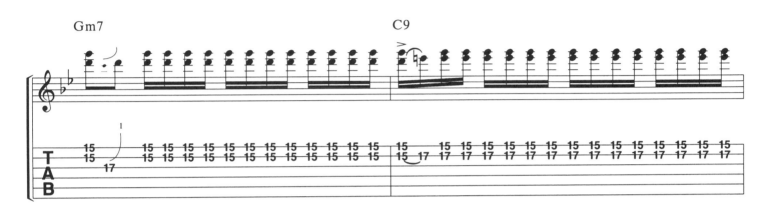

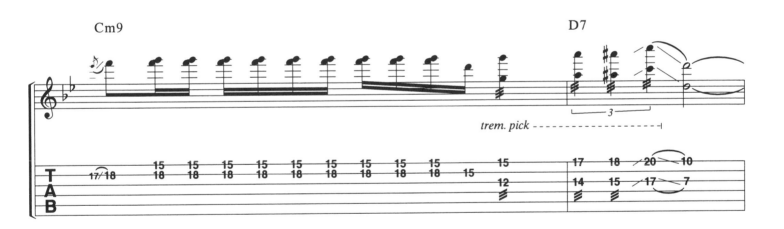

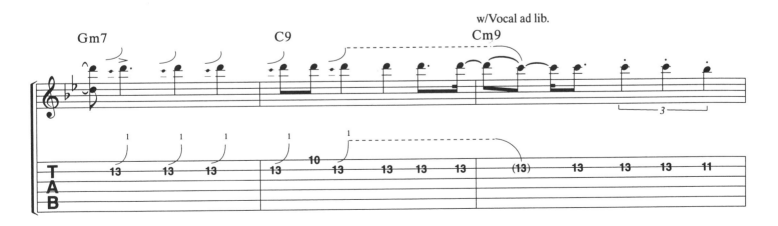

Outro:
w/Rhy. Fig. 2 *(Elec. Piano) 11 times, simile*
w/Lead Fig. 2 *(Elec. Gtr. 2) 11 times, simile*

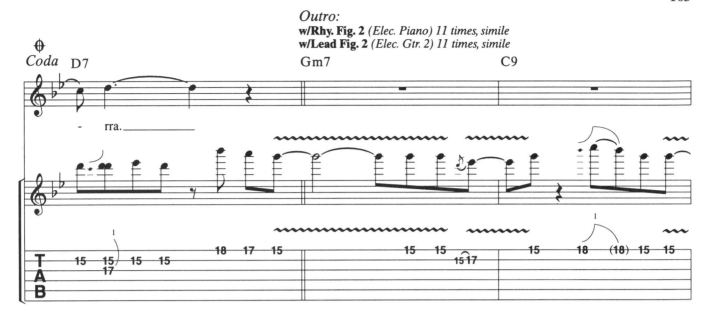

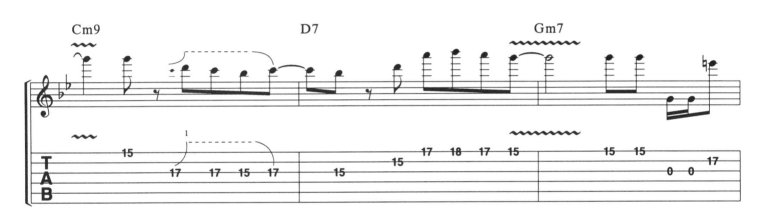

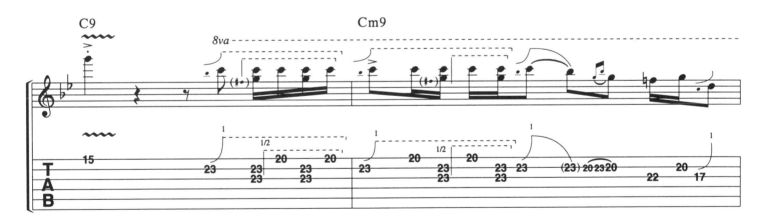

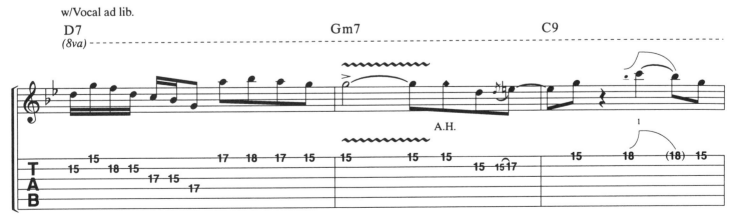

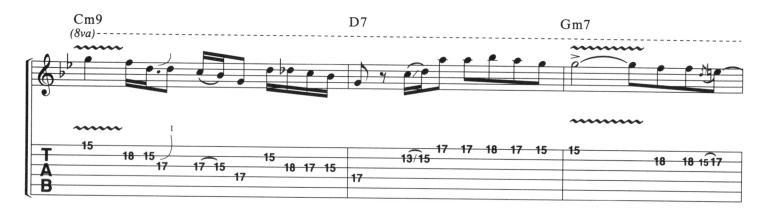

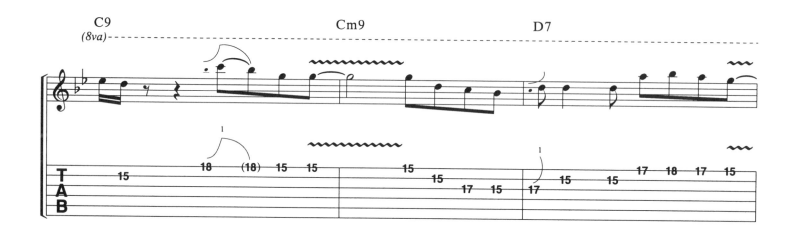

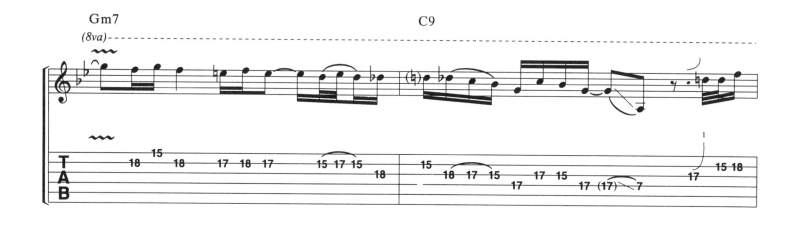

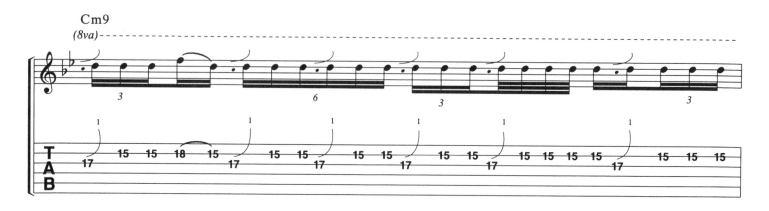

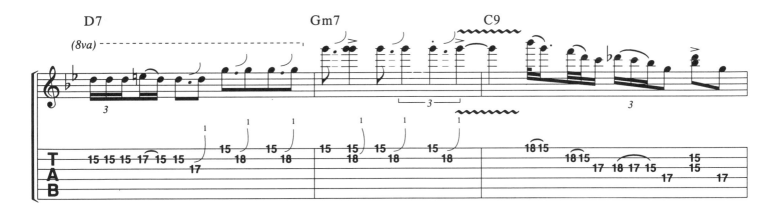

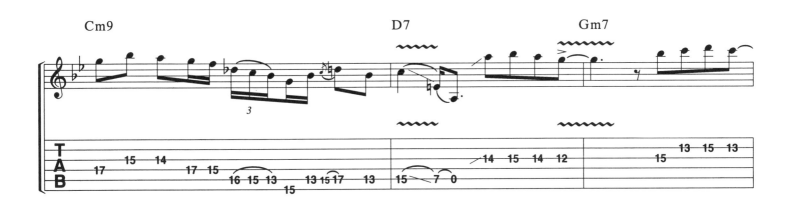

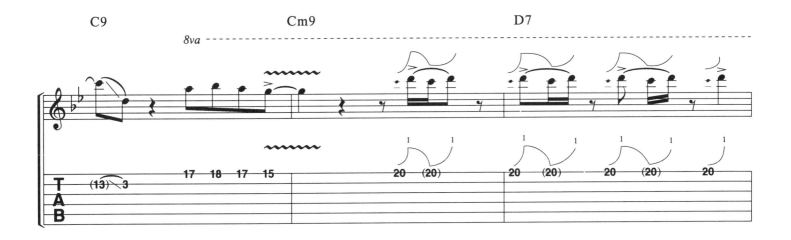

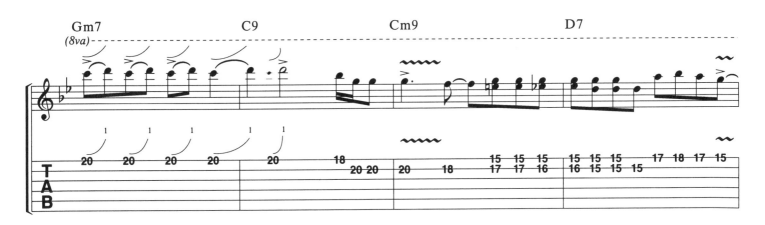

THE CALLING

**Words and Music by
CARLOS SANTANA, CHESTER THOMPSON
and LARRY GRAHAM**

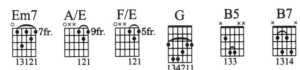

Moderately ♩ = 98
Intro:
Freely

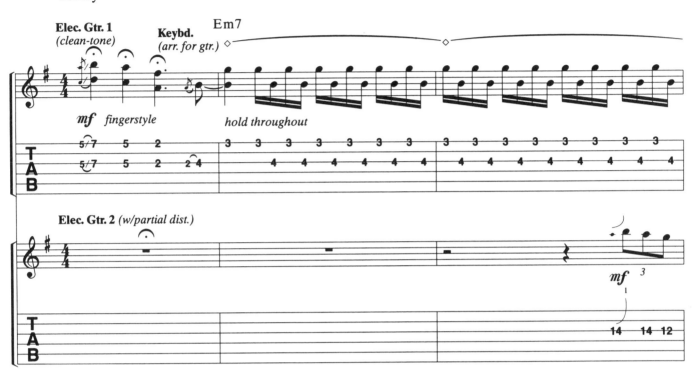

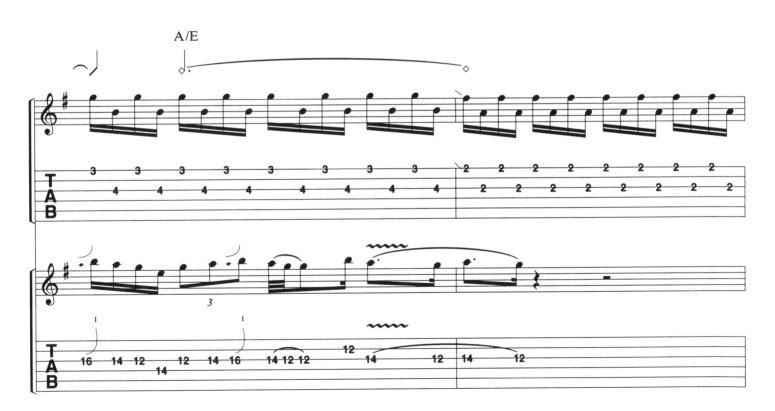

The Calling - 24 - 1
0413B

Em7

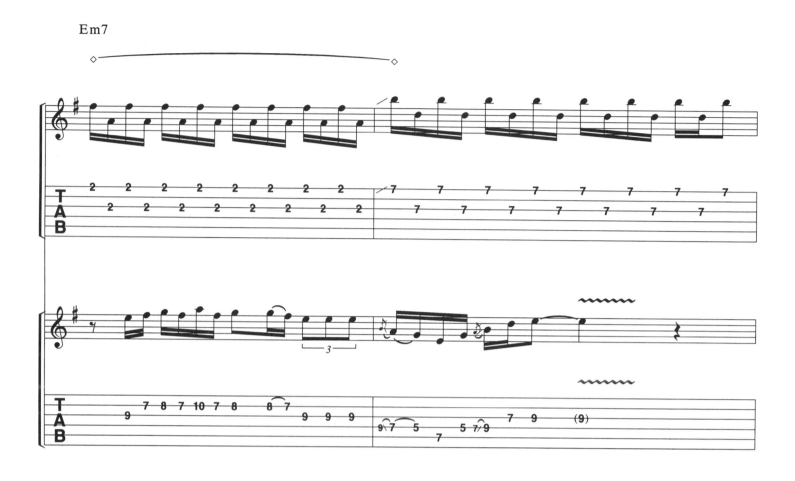

F/E

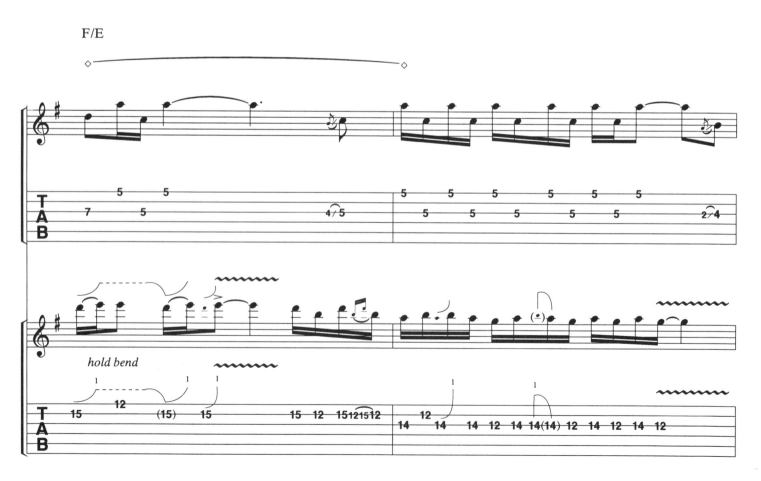

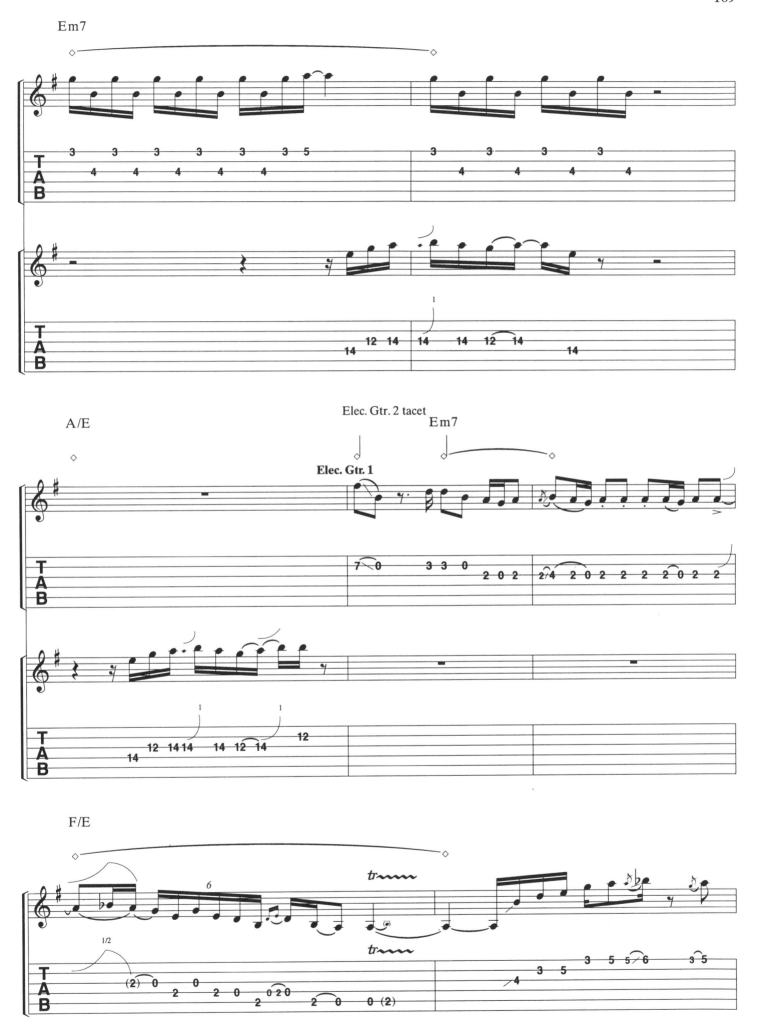

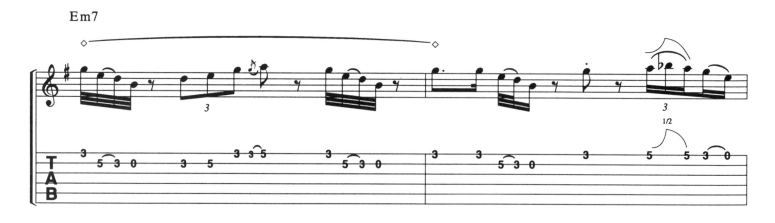

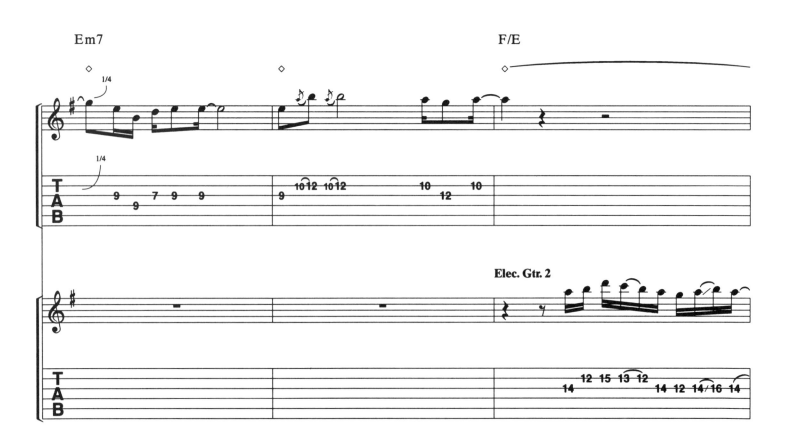

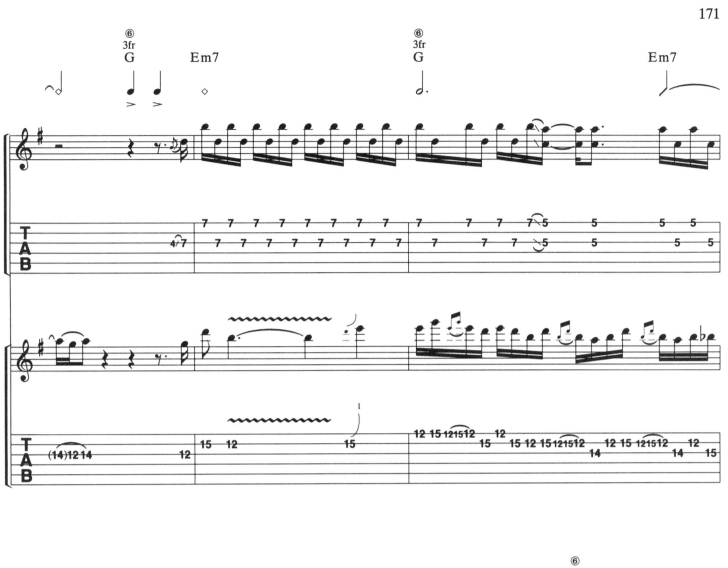

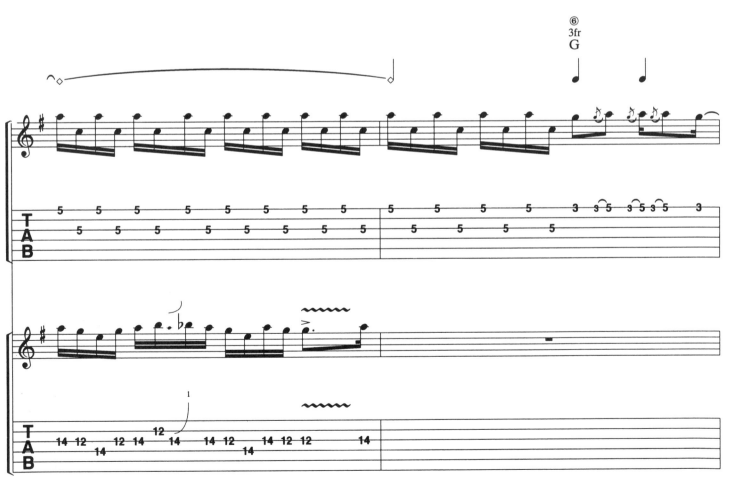

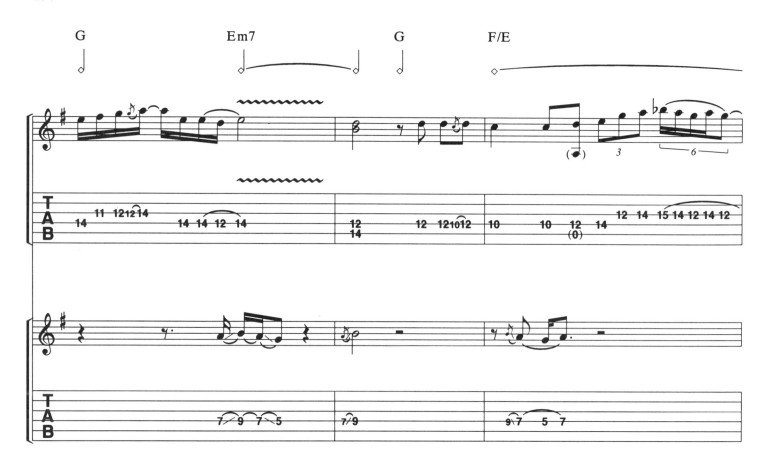

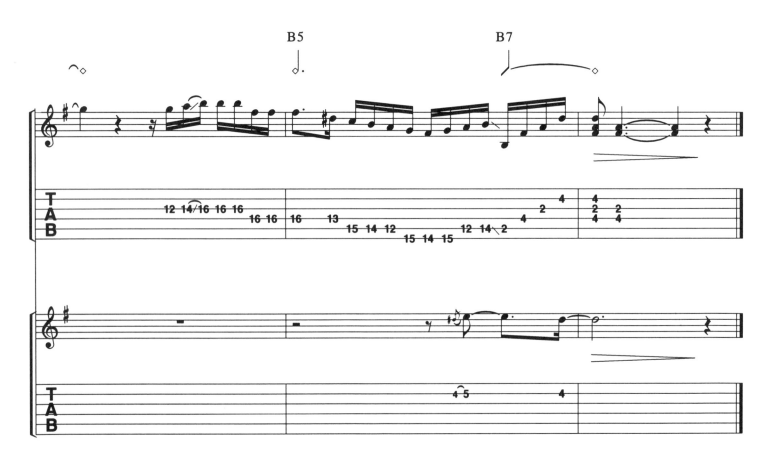

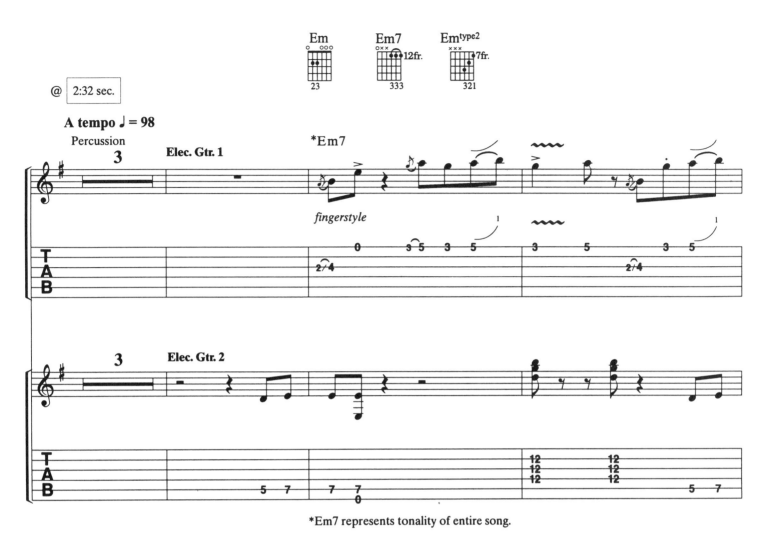

*Em7 represents tonality of entire song.

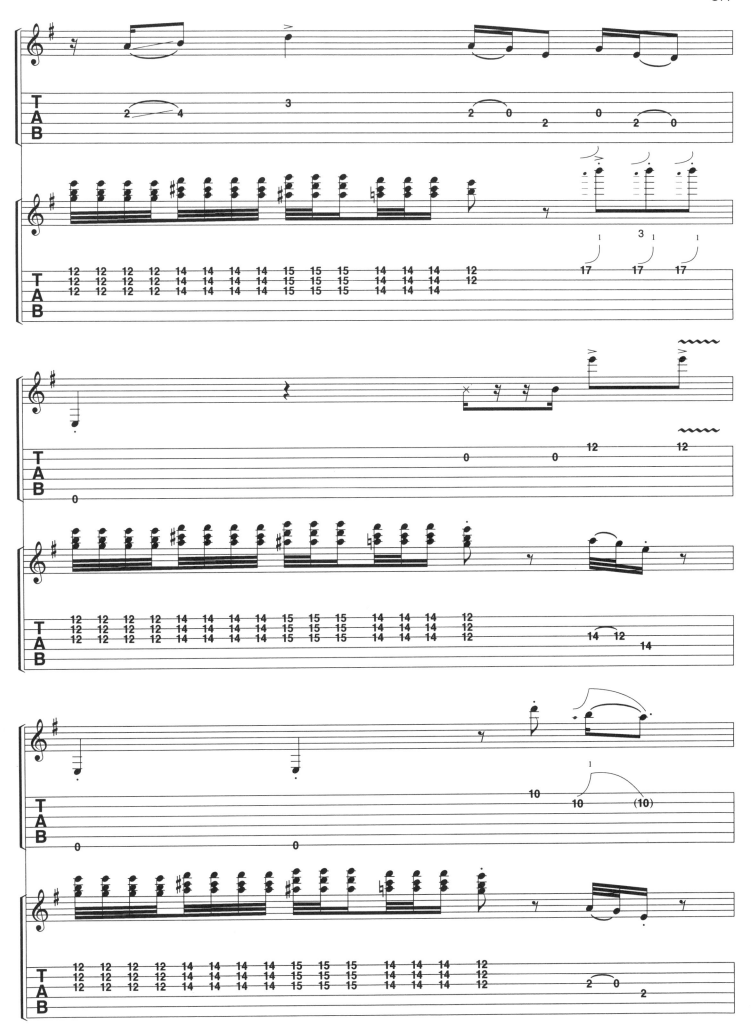

To Coda ⊕

Vocal Fig. 1

Peo - ple,   peo - ple,_____

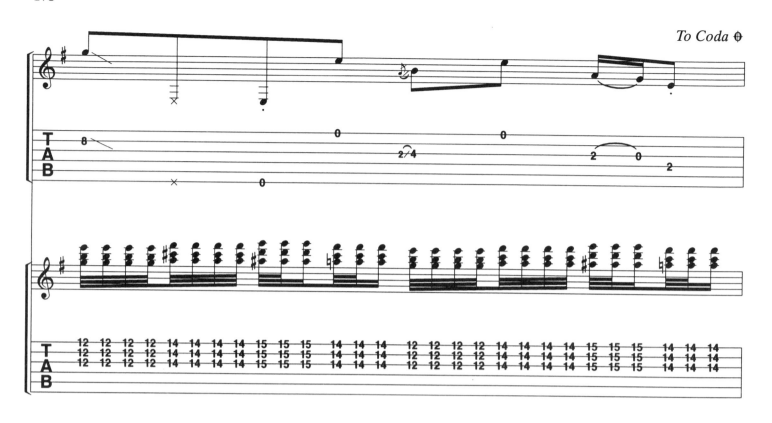

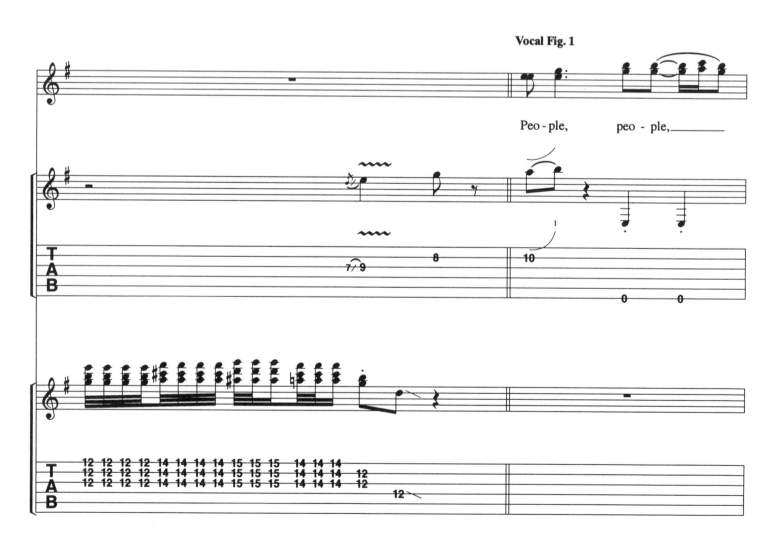

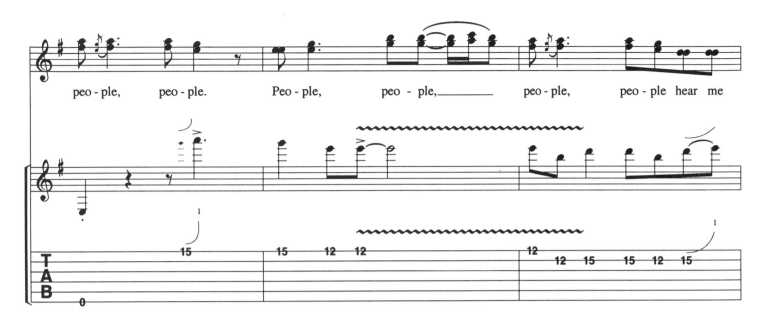

peo - ple, peo - ple. Peo - ple, peo - ple,_____ peo - ple, peo - ple hear me

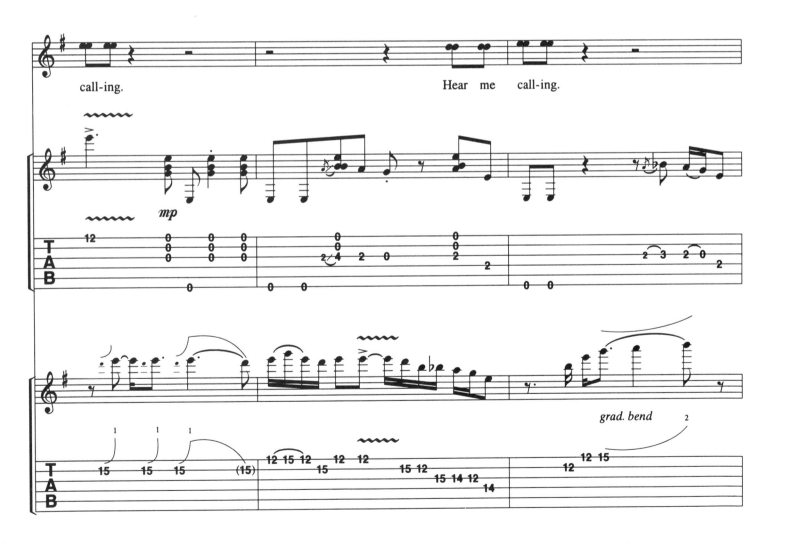

call-ing. Hear me call-ing.

grad. bend

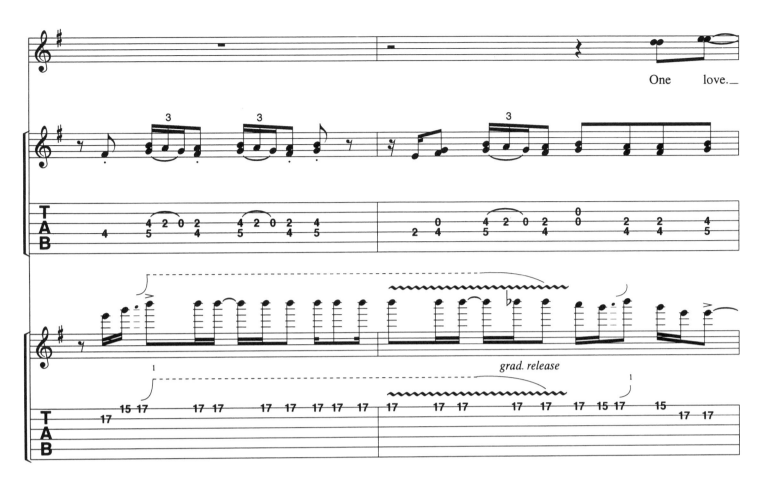

One   love.__

Gtrs. tacet
Percussion only

One love.__   Lord, God Al-might-y, one love.__

Elec. Gtr. 1

Elec. Gtr. 2

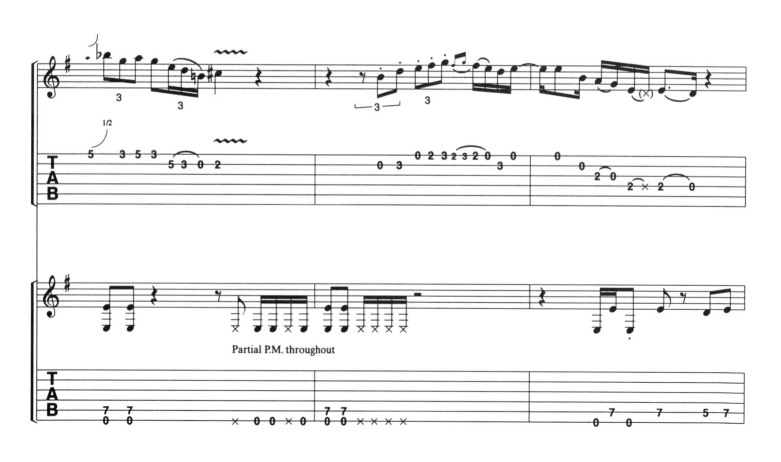

end partial P.M.

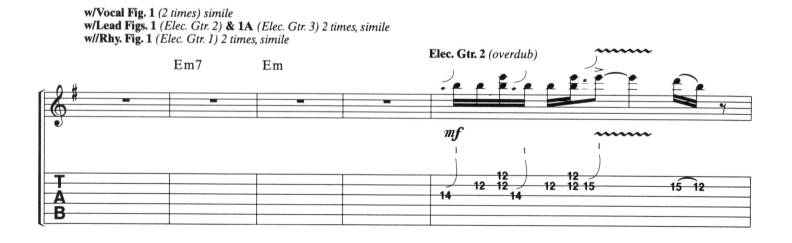

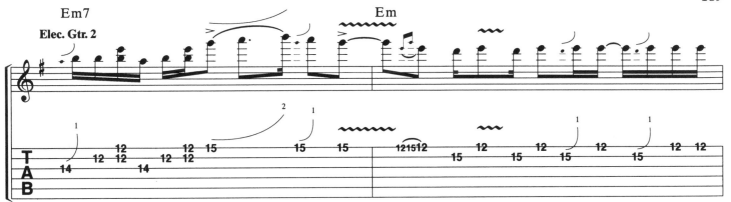

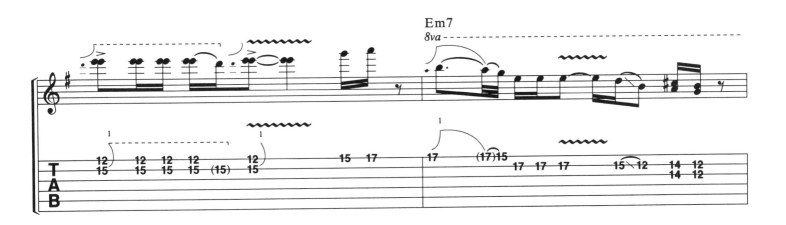

D.S. % al Coda

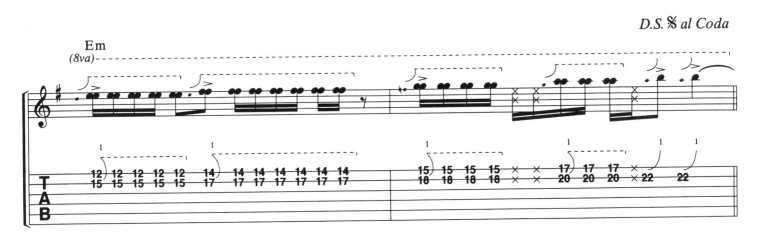

190

One love.

One love.

Lord, God Al-might-y, one love.

w/Rhy. Figs. 2 (Elec. Gtr. 2) & 2A (Elec. Gtr. 1) simile

Play 2 1/2 times and fade

One more.

One more.

The Calling - 24 - 24
0413B

GUITAR TAB GLOSSARY **

TABLATURE EXPLANATION

READING TABLATURE: Tablature illustrates the six strings of the guitar. Notes and chords are indicated by the placement of fret numbers on a given string(s).

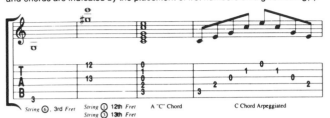

String ⑥, 3rd Fret   String ① 12th Fret   A "C" Chord   C Chord Arpeggiated
String ③ 13th Fret

BENDING NOTES

HALF STEP: Play the note and bend string one half step.*

PREBEND (Ghost Bend): Bend to the specified note, before the string is picked.

WHOLE STEP: Play the note and bend string one whole step.

PREBEND AND RELEASE: Bend the string, play it, then release to the original note.

WHOLE STEP AND A HALF: Play the note and bend string a whole step and a half.

REVERSE BEND: Play the already-bent string, then immediately drop it down to the fretted note.

SLIGHT BEND (Microtone): Play the note and bend string slightly to the equivalent of half a fret.

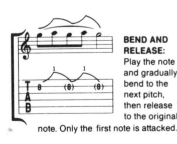

BEND AND RELEASE: Play the note and gradually bend to the next pitch, then release to the original note. Only the first note is attacked.

*A half step is the smallest interval in Western music; it is equal to one fret. A whole step equals two frets.

UNISON BEND: Play both notes and immediately bend the lower note to the same pitch as the higher note.

DOUBLE NOTE BEND: Play both notes and immediately bend both strings simultaneously.

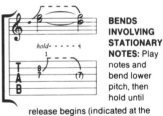

BENDS INVOLVING MORE THAN ONE STRING: Play the note and bend string while playing an additional note (or notes) on another string(s). Upon release, relieve pressure from additional note(s), causing original note to sound alone.

BENDS INVOLVING STATIONARY NOTES: Play notes and bend lower pitch, then hold until release begins (indicated at the point where line becomes solid).

TREMOLO BAR

SPECIFIED INTERVAL: The pitch of a note or chord is lowered to a specified interval and then may or may not return to the original pitch. The activity of the tremolo bar is graphically represented by peaks and valleys.

UN-SPECIFIED INTERVAL: The pitch of a note or a chord is lowered to an unspecified interval.

HARMONICS

NATURAL HARMONIC: A finger of the fret hand lightly touches the note or notes indicated in the tab and is played by the pick hand.

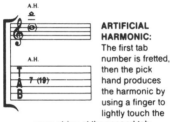

ARTIFICIAL HARMONIC: The first tab number is fretted, then the pick hand produces the harmonic by using a finger to lightly touch the same string at the second tab number (in parenthesis) and is then picked by another finger.

ARTIFICIAL "PINCH" HAR-MONIC: A note is fretted as indicated by the tab, then the pick hand produces the harmonic by squeezing the pick firmly while using the tip of the index finger in the pick attack. If parenthesis are found around the fretted note, it does not sound. No parenthesis means both the fretted note and A.H. are heard simultaneously.

© 1990 Beam Me Up Music
c/o CPP/Belwin, Inc. Miami, Florida 33014
International Copyright Secured   Made in U.S.A.   All Rights Reserved

**By Kenn Chipkin and Aaron Stang

RHYTHM SLASHES

STRUM INDICA-TIONS: Strum with indicated rhythm.

The chord voicings are found on the first page of the transcription underneath the song title.

INDICATING SINGLE NOTES USING RHYTHM SLASHES: Very often single notes are incorporated into a rhythm part. The note name is indicated above the rhythm slash with a fret number and a string indication.

ARTICULATIONS

HAMMER ON: Play lower note, then "hammer on" to higher note with another finger. Only the first note is attacked.

LEFT HAND HAMMER: Hammer on the first note played on each string with the left hand.

PULL OFF: Play higher note, then "pull off" to lower note with another finger. Only the first note is attacked.

FRET-BOARD TAPPING: "Tap" onto the note indicated by + with a finger of the pick hand, then pull off to the following note held by the fret hand.

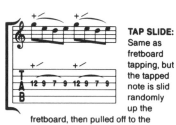

TAP SLIDE: Same as fretboard tapping, but the tapped note is slid randomly up the fretboard, then pulled off to the following note.

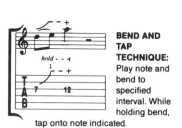

BEND AND TAP TECHNIQUE: Play note and bend to specified interval. While holding bend, tap onto note indicated.

LEGATO SLIDE: Play note and slide to the following note. (Only first note is attacked).

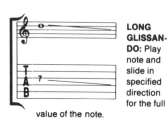

LONG GLISSAN-DO: Play note and slide in specified direction for the full value of the note.

SHORT GLISSAN-DO: Play note for its full value and slide in specified direction at the last possible moment.

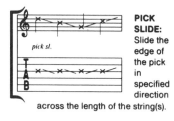

PICK SLIDE: Slide the edge of the pick in specified direction across the length of the string(s).

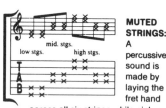

MUTED STRINGS: A percussive sound is made by laying the fret hand across all six strings while pick hand strikes specified area (low, mid, high strings).

PALM MUTE: The note or notes are muted by the palm of the pick hand by lightly touching the string(s) near the bridge.

TREMOLO PICKING: The note or notes are picked as fast as possible.

TRILL: Hammer on and pull off consecutively and as fast as possible between the original note and the grace note.

ACCENT: Notes or chords are to be played with added emphasis.

STACCATO (Detached Notes): Notes or chords are to be played roughly half their actual value and with separation.

DOWN STROKES AND UPSTROKES: Notes or chords are to be played with either a downstroke (⊓) or upstroke (∨) of the pick.

VIBRATO: The pitch of a note is varied by a rapid shaking of the fret hand finger, wrist, and forearm.

Printed and bound in Great Britain 10/00